The Black History A Look Back At The 20th Century Quiz Book

Melvett Chambers

Black History Quiz Book

A look back at the 20th century

The Black History Quiz Book, books are available at special quantity discounts when purchased in bulk by organizations, groups or corporations.

Library of Congress Control Number 2005900133

ISBN: 1-890994-39-1
Printed in the United States of America

Published by
Melvett Chambers
P.O. Box 10826
Midwest City, OK 73140

CONTENTS

Introduction

Presented in the *Black History Quiz Book; A Look Back At The 20th Century*, are some of the most important and impressive achievements and contributions made by Black Americans to America's culture and history. Quite frankly, there is so much to know about Black Americans that it would be impossible to provide anything truly exhaustive in one book such as this. It would be impossible to include every Black American worthy of note within the covers of this or any single volume. The extent to which Black Americans have contributed to every aspect of America's history and culture is immeasurable.

The Black American legacy is deeply stamped into the fabric of America. From Civil Rights and Political Leaders–Thurgood Marshall, the first Black American U.S. Supreme Court justice, founder of the NAACP's legal Defense and Educational Fund, lawyer whose victory in Brown v. Board of Education (1954) outlawed segregation in American public life;–Musicians and Singers,–after World War II, millions of Black Americans migrated from the rural South to large industrial cities in the North, such as Chicago and brought with them the traditional Blues of the Mississippi Delta, the music believed to be the true roots of all American music. It would be transformed into a new urban blues by some of the great blues artists such as Muddy Waters, Howlin' Wolf, Sonny Boy Williamson and many more;–Inventors, Scientists and Medicine,–rarely have they been acknowledged for the innovations and contributions that they have made to help change and enhance Americans life in the 20th Century such as George Washington Carver, the agricultural genius or Charles R. Drew, who's work with blood plasma and blood storage led to the development of the blood bank and a multitude of others;–Sports–Jackie Robinson, who changed the face of professional sports forever when he made his debut with the Brooklyn Dodgers on April 15, 1947, breaking the color barrier to Black Americans participation in professional sports. One could say, he set the table for so many who came to dinner,–Military–Actors and Writers.

The *Black History Quiz Book*, is designed to inform as well as entertain, inspire, motivate and challenge, focusing on the twentieth century, the past 100 years, 1900 - 1999. There is something in the *Black History Quiz Book* for everyone, young and old, history buff, or if history is not "your thang", it will be after reading this book.

The *Black History Quiz Book; A Look Back At The 20th Century*, was written to create a refreshed sense of pride–reverence and honor–to trailblazers of the past and present as we move into a new millennium. We thank them for their gifts of extraordinary courage, strength, hope, long-suffering, patients, endurance and love. Perhaps we can glean the essence of their spirit from the past and present and continue to challenge the negative stereotypes, myths and lies, progressing toward fulfilling the desires of the heart.

It's so important that we hold onto these things that are so real, when we're living in a society that has so much falsehood. "One has no knowledge of where they're going, if they don't know where they came from."

Acknowledgments

To my mother Mattie Chambers whose spirit of love and grace are forever with me. To my children Rosalind and Damon, I am grateful for the love, joy and purpose you bring into my life. A special thank to my wife Andrea. To Evelyn and Arnell Halstied whose constant encouragement and support have been unwavering over the years. Evelyn (Mom) thanks for your editing suggestions. To Palecia Lewis (Aunt) thanks for your encouragement, support and editing suggestions.

Many thanks to those who contributed to the making of this book, there are always so many people to thank whenever one undertakes a project of this magnitude. I wish to acknowledge all who contributed their thoughts and support. Thank you ever so much.

PHOTO CREDITS

Photos from Library of Congress are found on pages: 18, 21, 31, 43, 51, 54, 57, 61, 64, 68, 76, 79, 94, 111, 121, 129 and 147.

Photos from Melvett Chambers are found on pages: 14, 39, 40, 71, 127, 142, and 157.

Permission for use, United States Postal Service pages: 24, 25, 26 and 27.

Photo of General Colin Powell courtesy of General Colin Powell, page 59.

Photo of Admiral J. Paul Reason courtesy of United States Department of Defense, page 44.

Photo of Kareem Abdul-Jabbar/Melvett Chambers courtesy of William Morrow, page 83.

Photo of Bill Pickett courtesy of Denver Public Library, Western History Collection, page 97.

1900 - 1999

Time line of Important Events 1900 - 1999

1900

August 23 - The National Negro Business League, sponsored by Booker T. Washington was formed in Boston.

1901

March 4 - George H. White left Congress. It would be more than twenty years before another Black American served in Congress.

1902

Robert H. Terrell was the first Black justice of the peace, as judges of municipal court were called then, which made him the first federal judge at any level.

1903

Maggie Lena Walker was the first Black woman bank president. She founded the Saint Luke Penny Saving Bank in Richmond, Virginia.

1904

Charles Young was the first Black military attaché in the history of the United States.

1905

Robert S. Abbott began publication of the militant Chicago Defender. It became one of the most widely read and influential Black newspaper in the country.

1906

June - John Hope assumed the Presidency of Morehouse College. Hope, one of the most militant of early Black educators, was the school's first Black and the catalyst behind many of the programs that resulted in Morehouse's favorable reputation.

1907

Alain Leroy Locke, one of the most brilliant Black American intellectuals, was awarded a Rhodes Scholarship, which he used to continue studying at Oxford University in England and the University of Berlin in Germany. He was the first Black Rhodes Scholar. It was not until 1960 that the second Black Rhodes scholar, Joseph S. Sanders, was selected.

1908

December 26 - Jack Johnson knocked out Tommy Burns in Sidney, Australia, in the fourteenth round to become the first Black heavyweight boxing champion.

1909

February 12 - The National Association for the Advancement of Colored People (NAACP), was founded in New York City, New York.

April 6 - Admiral Peary accompanied by Black American, Matthew Henson, discovered the North Pole.

1910

November - The *Crisis* magazine debuts. W.E.B. Du Bois is its first editor, the magazine became the NAACP's official voice.

1911

April - The National Urban League is founded in New York City, New York. The new organization stresses employment and industrial opportunities for Black American.

November 26 - William Henry Lewis was the first Black American appointed to a sub-cabinet post. President William Howard Taft appointed his assistant attorney general of the United States.

1912

James Weldon Johnson's *The Autobiography of an Ex-Colored Man* is published. It spurred white recognition of Black culture and the advent of the Harlem Renaissance.

1913

Daniel Hale Williams was a founder and vice-president of the National Medical Association, and the first and only Black American invited to become a charter member of the American College of Surgeons.

1914

The Spingarn Medal Awards are instituted by Joel E. Spingarn, chairman of the board of directors of the NAACP, to distinguish merit and achievement of Black American.

1915

September 9 - Carter G. Woodson founded the Association for the Study of Negro Life and History (ASNLH).

1916

Carter G. Woodson published the first issue of the *Journal of Negro History*, the first Black American historical research journal.

1917

April 6 - the United States formally enters World War I. Some 370,000 Black Americans join the military, and more than half of the Black Americans served in the French war zone.

1918

November 11 - World War I officially ends. The "Great Migration" of Black American to industrial centers of the North began in earnest during the war.

1919

Frederick Douglass "Fritz" Pollard, became the first Black player-coach in professional football when he joined the Akron Indians of the American Professional Football Association.

1920

August 1 - Marcus Garvey's Universal Improvement Association holds its national convention in Harlem. Garvey's Black nationalist movement was the first Black American mass movement.

1921

January - The Pace Phonograph Company, which used the Black Swan label, was the first Black American owned and operated record company. It was established by Harry Pace.

1922

Henry W. Shields was elected to the legislature as a Democrat. He was the first Black American, Democrat elected to any political office.

1923

Garrett A. Morgan patents his automatic traffic signal invention. He later sells his patent to the General Electric Company.

1924

The first World Series between Negro League clubs was held. Leagues from this period included the National Negro Baseball League, the American Association League, the Mid-Western Baseball League, and the Negro International League.

1925
George H. Woodson became the first Black American president of the Negro Bar Association (now the National Bar Association), an organization formed to forward the concerns of Black Lawyers.

1926
Negro History Week, (now Black History Month) is introduced by Carter G. Woodson.

1927
In the case of Nixon v. Herndon, the United States Supreme Court, strikes down the Texas law that bars Black American from voting in white only primaries.

1928
Oscar De Priest, a Republican is the first Black American elected to Congress since Reconstruction.

1929
The first two full-length films with all Black casts were *Hearts in Dixie*, starring Nina Mae McKinney, Daniel Haynes, and Victoria Spivey; and *Hallilujah*, starring Stepin Fetchit, Clarence Muse, and Mildred Washington.

1930
President Herbert Hoover nominates Judge John J. Parker of North Carolina to the United States Supreme court. The NAACP successfully leads a campaign against Parker's confirmation.

1931
March 30 - Nine Black youths are arrested and returned to Scottsboro, Alabama for allegedly raping two white women. They are quickly convicted in a trial that outrages Blacks and much of the nation.

1932
The *Atlanta Daily World*, the first Black newspaper in modern times began publishing daily.

1933
Charles Alfred Anderson and Albert E. Forsythe were the first Black American pilots to make a transcontinental flight.

1934
Arthur W. Mitchell was the first Black Democrat elected to the United States Congress. He defeated Republican Congressman Oscar De Priest.

1935
The National Council of Negro Women is founded by Mary McLeod Bethune. She became its first president, a post she held until 1949.

1936
Jesse Owens wins four gold medals in the Olympic Games held in Germany, challenging Adolf Hitler's notions of superior Aryan race and the inferiority of Black American athletes.

1937
William H. Hastie is confirmed as judge of the United States District Court in the Virgin Islands.

1938
Crystal Bird Faucet of Philadelphia became the country's first Black female legislator when she was elected to the Pennsylvania House of Representatives.

1939
Jane Bolin is appointed judge of the Court of Domestic Relations in New York City by Mayor Fiorello LaGuardia, becoming the first female judge in the United States.

1940
Benjamin O. Davis, Sr. is the first Black American to be appointed brigadier general in the history of the United States.

1941
December 7 - The Japanese attack the United States Naval Base at Pearl Harbor. The United States enters World War II.

Dorie Miller, a messman aboard the USS *Arizona* mans a machine gun during the Pearl Harbor attack, downs four enemy planes and is awarded the Navy Cross.

1942
The Congress of Racial Equality (CORE), a Civil Rights group dedicated to a direct action, non-violent program, is founded.

1943
Smith v. Allwright, a major Black voting rights case, reaches the United States Supreme Court.

1944
The USS *Harmon* was the first fighting ship named after a Black American, Leonard Roy Harmon. Harmon was a World War II naval hero. He was awarded the Navy Cross.

April 25 - The United Negro College Fund is established.

1945
November 1– The first issue of Ebony magazine was published by Johnson Publishing Company of Chicago. John H. Johnson is the company founder and editor.

1946
November 1 - Dr. Charles S. Johnson became the first Black American president of Fisk University.

1947
April 10 - Jackie Robinson joined the Brooklyn Dodgers and became the first Black American in the 20th century to play in major league baseball.

1948
September 18 - Ralph J. Bunche is appointed by the United Nations Security Council, acting United Nations mediator in Palestine.

1949
October 3 - William Henry Hastie is appointed to the United States District Court of Appeals. He is the first Black American to sit on the court.

1950
September 22 - Ralph J. Bunche was awarded the Nobel Peace Prize for his successful mediation of the Israeli-Palestine conflict. He was the first Black American to win a Nobel Prize.

1951

The 24th Infantry Regiment, last all Black unit in the United States Army, is disbanded after seeing action in the Korean War.

1952

Charlotta A. Bass, political activist and editor of *The California Eagle*, is the first Black American woman to run for vice-president of the United States.

1953

December 31 - Hulan Jack became the first Black president of a Borough in Manhattan.

1954

May 17 - The United States Supreme Court in *Brown v. Board of Education* decision declared segregation in public schools unconstitutional.

1955

December 1 - Rosa Parks, a seamstress is arrested after she refused to give her seat to a white man on a Montgomery, Ala. Bus. Her arrest sparks the Montgomery Bus Boycott.

1956

Entertainer Nat King Cole became the first Black American to host his own television show, The Nat King Cole Show.

February 3 - Autherine Lucy is admitted to the University of Alabama by court order. She was suspended February 7 after a riot at the University.

1957

July 6 - Althea Gibson became the first Black American tennis player to win the singles title at Wimbledon, England.

August 29 - Congress passed the Civil Rights Act of 1957, the first federal civil rights legislation since 1875.

1958

Clifford R. Wharton, Sr., became minister to Romania, the first Black American to head an American embassy in Europe.

1959

Brigadier General Benjamin O. Davis, Jr., of the United States Air Force is promoted to major general, the highest military rank yet achieved by an Black American.

1960
Wilma Rudolph is the first Black American woman to win three gold medals at the Olympic Games, held in Rome, Italy.

1961
College football's Heisman Trophy is awarded to Ernie Davis, a halfback for Syracuse University, the first time the Heisman has been given to an Black American.

1962
January 31 - Lt. Commander Samuel Lee Gravely, Jr. was given command of the destroyer escort USS *Falgout*. This was the first time in modern navy history that a Black American had been given command of a U.S. warship.

1963
June 12 - Medger W. Evers, NAACP field secretary in Mississippi, was assassinated in front of his Jackson, Mississippi home.

1964
December 10 - The Nobel Peace Prize is awarded to Dr. Martin Luther King, Jr., at ceremonies held in Oslo, Norway.

1965
President Johnson signs the Voting Rights Act of 1965, letting federal agents register Black American voters if state agents refuse to do so.

1966
January 18 - Robert C. Weaver is sworn in as Secretary of Housing and Urban Development, he was appointed by President Lyndon B. Johnson, and became the first Black American cabinet member.

November 8 - Edward L. Brooke of Massachusetts is the first Black American elected to the United States Senate since Reconstruction.

1967
President Lyndon B. Johnson appoints U.S. Solicitor General Thurgood Marshall, associate justice of the United States Supreme Court. Marshall was confirmed by the U.S. Senate on August 30, and became the first Black American United States Supreme Court Justice.

1968
April 4 - Dr. Martin Luther King is assassinated by a sniper in Memphis, TN.

1969

October 17 - Clifton Reginald Wharton, Jr., is appointed president of Michigan State University. He is the first Black American to head a major, predominantly White university in the 20th Century.

1970

June 23 - Charles Rangel defeated Adam Clayton Powell and replaced him in Congress, representing Harlem.

November 3 - Twelve Black Americans Democrats are elected to the 92nd Congress.

1971

April 28 - Samuel L. Gravely, Jr. became the first Black American admiral in the United States Navy.

1972

April 19 - Major General Frederick E. Davidson assumed command of the Eight Infantry Division in Germany, to become the first Black American to lead an U.S. Army division.

1973

Black Americans mayors are elected in major United States cities, including Thomas Bradley in Los Angeles, Coleman Young in Detroit and Maynard Jackson in Atlanta.

1974

April 8 - Hank Aaron hit home run number 715 in a game at Atlanta Stadium against the Los Angeles Dodgers, to break Babe Ruth's major league baseball record.

1975

September 1 - General Daniel "Chappie" James, Jr., is the first Black American to be promoted to the rank of four star general, and named commander-in-chief of the North American Air Defense Command (NORAD).

1976

Benjamin Hooks, named to succeed Roy Wilkins as executive director of the NAACP.

1977

November 12 - Ernest N. Morial was sworn in as the first Black American

Mayor of New Orleans.

1978

January 16 - National Aeronautics and Space Administration, (NASA) named three Black American astronauts, Major Frederick D. Gregory, Major Guion S. Bluford and Dr. Ronald E. McNair.

1979

July 19 - Patricia R. Harris, formerly the United States Secretary of Housing and Urban Development, is named the Secretary of Health, Education and Welfare.

1980

January 25 - Robert L. Johnson established the first Black American oriented cable television network, Black Entertainment Television (BET). It marked the first time that Black viewers had access to quality Black programming.

1981

President Ronald Reagan appointed Clarence Pendleton, Jr., to replace Arthur S. Flemming as chairman of the United States commission on Civil Rights. Pendleton became the first Black American to chair the Civil Rights Commission.

1982

August 11 - United States Army Lt. General Roscoe Robinson Jr. was promoted to four-star general, making his the second Black American in the U.S. military history to achieve that rank.

1983

October 19 - The United States Senate, by a vote of 78 - 22, designates the third Monday in January of each year a federal holiday in honor of Dr. Martin Luther King Jr.

1984

Levi Watkins, Jr. was the first Black American doctor to establish the surgical implantation of an automatic defibrillator in the human heart.

1985

January 4 - United States Congressman, William H. Gray was elected chairman of the House Budget Committee. This was the highest rank ever reached by a Black American Congressman.

1986
Oprah Winfrey is the first Black American woman to host a nationally syndicated weekday talk show, "The Oprah Winfrey Show".

1987
The National Aeronautics and Space Administration, (NASA) space program, selects Mae C. Jemison as an astronaut, making her the first Black American woman astronaut.

1988
September 6 - Lee Roy Young became the first Black American to be a Texas Ranger in the police force's 165 year existence.

1989
General Colin L. Powell became the first Black American to be appointed chairperson of the United States Joint Chiefs of Staff, the nation's highest military post.

Art Shell of the Oakland Raiders became the first Black American, head coach in the NFL.

1990
Denzel Washington wins an Academy Award for Best Actor for *Glory*.

Charles Johnson wins the National Book Award for his novel "*The Middle Passage*".

1991
Clarence Thomas is selected to replace Thurgood Marshall, who retired from the United States Supreme Court, despite the opposition of civil rights groups and allegations of sexual harassment brought by former colleague Anita Hill.

1992
Carol Moseley-Braun of Illinois is the first Black American woman elected to the United States Senate.

1993
Martin Luther King, Jr., Day is celebrated in all 50 states for the first time since it was created as a national holiday in 1983. It is observe on the third Monday in January.

1994
Len Coleman is named president of baseball's National League.

1995
More than one-million Black American men gather in Washington, DC for the Million Man March, organized by the Nation of Islam's Louis Farrakhan.

1996
Texaco settles the largest discrimination case in U.S. history, when it agreed to pay $176 million to 1,400 current and former Black American employees.

1997
Tiger Woods becomes the first Black/Asian American to win a major golf tournament with his record breaking victory in the Masters.

Eddie Robinson retires as coach of Grambling State football team after 57 seasons and a record 408 victories.

1998
The President's Commission on Race, led by John Hope Franklin, pursues a national dialogue on issues affecting Black Americans.

1999
Lauryn Hill grabs five Grammy Awards, including Album of The Year and Best New Artist. The 23 year-old soul diva breaks Carole King's 1971 record for most awards nabbed by a female artist in a single night.

June 15 - President Bill Clinton presents the Congressional Gold Medal to Rosa Parks.

September 12 - Serena Williams and her sister Venus Williams became the first Black American women's team to succeed at the U.S. Open in New York city. They won the doubles title 4 - 6, 6 - 1, 6 - 4.

History

History

1. Lawyer and businessman who managed the largest Black owned firm in the United States. In 1987 I orchestrated the largest leveraged buyout in business history, paying $985 million for Beatrice International Food. With subsidiaries in almost every continent, the renamed TLC Beatrice International became the largest Black-owned firm in the United States. I gave generously to many charities. My gift of three million to Harvard Law School in 1992 was the largest single gift the law school had received. A center at Harvard was the first facility named for an Black American. Who Am I?

2. In December of 1955, 42,000 Black American residents of Montgomery, Alabama began a year-long boycott of city buses, that galvanized the American Civil Rights Movement and led to a 1956 United States Supreme Court decision declaring segregated seating on buses unconstitutional. This boycott was known as what?

3. In 1905 W.E.B. DuBois, William Monroe Trotter, and other Black militants founded the Niagara Movement, an organization committed to securing full citizenship rights for Black American. The Niagara Movement was short-lived, but its goals were adopted by an organization, founded in New York in 1909 by an interracial group of reformers and Civil Rights activists. What is the name of this organization?

4. After a successful basketball career with the Detroit Pistons, and other teams, I entered the business world in 1980 and achieved success by manufacturing components for the automobile industry. My firm employs 500 men and women. Who Am I?

5. I was a member of the 1909 expedition with American explorer Robert Peary, who is generally credited with discovering the North Pole. In 1912, I wrote "*A Black Explorer at The North Pole*". In 1913, President Taft personally recommended my appointment to the United States Customs House in New York City

Answers on page 46

In recognition of my exploits in the Arctic. In 1986, I was commemorated on a U.S. postage stamp. Who Am I?

6. I developed the Schomburg Center for Research in Black Culture into the world's largest collection of materials by and about people of African descent. I joined the staff of the New York Public Library in 1936. Twelve years later, I was appointed head of its Black American collection, the complete private library of Afro-Puerto Rican bibliophile, Arthur A. Schomburg, located on 135th Street and Lenox Avenue in Harlem. Under my leadership, the library's holdings grew from 15,000 books to its present collection of more than 5,000,000 separately catalogued items. Who Am I?

7. I was the founder and president of The Brotherhood of Sleeping Car Porters, cofounder and Editor of The Messenger, and architect of the March on Washington which led to the establishment of the Fair Employment Practices Committee, and the March on Washington DC in 1963. Who Am I?

8. I'm one of the most prominent Black American TV news commentators and anchormen. In 1967 I joined WCBS radio in New York. In 1971 CBS sent me to its Paris bureau and then to Vietnam, where I spent 18 months, leaving when I was wounded by mortar fire. I became anchorman on CBS Sunday Night News, the first Black American to hold that post and a panelist on "Sixty Minutes". My many awards include three Emmys. Who Am I?

9. This Black American women's magazine was founded in 1970, focusing on health, beauty, fashion, self-improvement, and issues of interest to contemporary upscale Black women. 50,000 copies of the magazine were published in 1970 by Clarence Smith and Edward Lewis, the first issue of a monthly magazine aimed at Black women in the post-civil rights era. What is the name of the magazine?

10. The leader from 1977 to 1997, and one of the founding members of the Southern Christian Leadership Conference (SCLC) in 1957, I was part of a core group of ministers, including Martin Luther King Jr., Fred Suttlesworth, and Ralph Abernathy, who were integral to the Civil Rights Movement of 1960s. Who Am I?

Answers on page 46

Matthew Alexander Henson

Did You Know

That Matthew Henson, one of the world's greatest explorers accompanied Lt. Robert Peary on all of his Arctic treks and was with him on the final attempt to reach the North Pole on April 6, 1909. Henson, Peary, and four Eskimos finally made it. Matthew Henson was actually the first man to reach the Pole, but was denied recognition for his role for years. Eventually, he did get the recognition he deserved. In 1944, Henson received a joint medal from the Congress of the United States. He was also honored by Presidents Truman and Eisenhower. In 1986, Henson was commemorated on a postage stamp.

11. An estimated 1.5 million Black American women seeking to build coalitions within the Black community, congregated on Philadelphia's Benjamin Franklin Parkway for the Million Woman March, under the slogan: "Repentance, Resurrection, and Restoration." What was the month, date and year of the March?

12. "If you must die, take at least one with you", was the slogan of this weekly newspaper, *The Chicago Defender*, founded on May 6, 1905. Under my direction, this newspaper became the most widely circulated Black American newspaper of its time and a leading voice in the fight against racism. Who Am I?

13. I was a historian and educator who pioneered the research of Black American history. In 1915, I established the Association for the Study of Negro Life and History (ASNLH), later named the Association for the Study of Afro-American Life and History. I founded the *Journal of Negro History* 1916, *the Associated Publishers* 1921, and the *Negro History Bulletin* 1937. The *Negro History Bulletin* provided elementary and secondary teachers lessons in Black American history.

One of my enduring achievements is my initiation of Black History Month. In 1926, I launched Negro History Week, a commemoration of Black American achievement held the second week of February, which marks the birthdays of Frederick Douglass and Abraham Lincoln. Negro History Week was renamed Black History Month in the 1960s. I published more than 20 books and countless articles, often referred to as the "Father of African-American studies." Who Am I?

14. I was the first Black American woman aviator and stunt-flyer. Every Memorial Day I am honored by Black American pilots who fly in formation above the Chicago Lincoln Cemetery and drop wreaths on my grave. In 1975, a group of Black women in Chicago interested in aviation and aerospace started a aviators organization in my name for my efforts in opening the field of aviation to Black Americans. I was commemorated on a United States postal stamp in 1995. Who Am I?

15. Throughout my career, I was committed to finding ways to use my expertise in social sciences for the cause of racial justice. In the early 1950s, I frequently served as an expert witness for the National

ANSWERS ON PAGE 46

Association for the Advancement of Colored People (NAACP). However, my greatest fame came as a result of my research on the self-image of Black children. I studied the responses of more than 200 Black children who were given a choice of white or brown dolls. My study showed that the children had a preference for the white dolls from as early as three years old. I concluded that segregation was psychologically damaging. This conclusion played a pivotal role in *"Brown v. Board of Education",* the Supreme Court case that outlawed segregated education. Who Am I?

16. The Million Man March emerged from Nation of Islam Minister Louis Farrakhan's call for a "Day of Atonement". What was the month, date, and year of the march?

17. I was one of the best known agricultural scientists of my generation. I was born into slavery near Diamond, Missouri. In 1923, I was awarded the prestigious Spingarn Medal, the highest annual award given by the National Association for the Advancement of Colored People (NAACP). I directed Tuskegee's agricultural research department until my death in 1943. I was buried beside my great friend and mentor, Booker T. Washington, on Tuskegee campus. My epitaph sums up my humanitarianism; "He could have added fortune to fame, but caring for neither, he found happiness and honor in being helpful to the world". Who Am I?

18. On December 1, 1955, in Montgomery, Alabama the arrest of this Black woman for disregarding an order to surrender her bus seat to a white passenger, galvanized a growing movement to desegregate public transportation and marked a historic turning point in the Black American battle for civil rights. I'm often called the "Mother of the Civil Rights Movement". Who Am I?

19. June 1997, when President Bill Clinton assembled a seven member panel to advise him about racial strife in the United States, he chose me as its chairman. Born in the all-Black Oklahoma frontier town of Rentiesville, my family moved to Tulsa in 1926. I received a B.A. from Fisk University in Nashville, Tennessee where I graduated with honors in 1935. I earned a doctorate in history from Harvard University six years later. Of my many books, *From Slavery to Freedom: A History of American Negroes*

Answers on page 46

Ralph J. Bunche

Did You Know

That Ralph Bunche (August 7, 1904 - December 9, 1971), an American diplomat and political scientist, whose role as the "architect" of the United Nations peacekeeping operations led to his winning the Nobel Peace Prize in 1950. Bunche became the first Black American so honored. His contributions as a scholar were recognized in 1953, when he was elected the first Black president of the American Political Science Association. In 1963, President Kennedy awarded Bunche the nation's highest civilian honor, the Medal of Freedom.

is the most famous. Since its publication in 1947, the book has gone through seven editions; the most recent is subtitled, *A History of African Americans*. Among the many organizations that I have headed are the American Historical Association, the American Studies Association, and the United Chapters of Phi Beta Kappa. I served as a delegate to the 21st General Conference of United Nations Educational Scientific and Cultural Organization in 1980. I have been inducted into the Oklahoma Hall of Fame, and have received the Presidential Metal of Freedom. Who Am I?

a. Asa Philip Randolph
b. John Hope Franklin
c. Martin Luther King, Jr.

20. I'm called by many the greatest American of the twentieth century, I was born in Atlanta, GA. My parents were members of the city's "Black establishment," my father was one of the city's leading Black ministers. I was educated at Morehouse College, Crozier Theological Seminary, and received my Ph.D. from Boston University in 1955. I began my ministerial career as pastor of the Dexter Avenue Baptist Church in Montgomery, Alabama in 1954. Who Am I?

a. Martin Luther King, Jr.
b. Carter Godwin Woodson
c. Booker T. Washington

21. I was one of the most brilliant Black American intellectuals, and in 1907, the recipient of a Rhodes Scholarship. It would be more than half a century before the next Black American would be selected for this distinguished academic honor. I obtained my Ph.D. from Harvard University in 1918. As a Rhodes Scholar, I studied at Oxford University in England from 1907 to 1910, and at the University of Berlin from 1910 to 1911. I became professor of philosophy at Howard University in 1912. Who Am I?

a. John Hope Franklin
b. Marcus Garvey
c. Alain Leroy Locke

ANSWERS ON PAGE 46

22. April 24, 1944, Frederick D. Patterson, President of Tuskegee Institute founded this organization, to coordinate the fundraising efforts for historically Black colleges and universities. What is the name of the organization?

23. April 5, 1953, this University received a chapter of Phi Beta Kappa, the prestigious scholastic honor society. In later years, only two other all Black schools, Howard and Morehouse Universities, were awarded chapters. What is the name of the university?

24. A major force in the radio industry, who can be heard daily on over 100 stations, I earned the nickname "The Hardest Working Man in Radio" and "The Fly Jock" by working long hours and flying between my morning job-in Dallas, Texas-and afternoon job-in Chicago, Illinois-every weekday for years. I am the host of a nationally syndicated morning radio show, graduated from Tuskegee University, founder of BlackAmericaWeb.com, Reach Media Incorporated and a Foundation that was started in 1998. The purpose of the Foundation is to support Black American students in need at Historically Black Colleges and Universities with scholarship assistance. The Foundation has raised more than 14 million and supported over 40 colleges and assisted thousands of students. Who Am I?
    a. Tony Brown
    b. Tom Joyner
    c. Robert L. Johnson

25. I joined the board of trustees of the Ford Foundation in 1977, and in 1979, I was elected president of the Ford Foundation, becoming the first Black American to head the country's largest philanthropic foundation. I have received a number of awards, including Columbia Law School's James Kent Medal for distinguished professional achievements and Columbia University's Medal of Excellence. Who Am I?
    a. Mahlon Martin
    b. Franklin A. Thomas
    c. Herbert Carter

ANSWERS ON PAGE 46

It wasn't until 1940 that the image of an Black American first appeared on a U.S. postage stamp, Booker T. Washington, who had founded Tuskegee Institute in 1881, became the first to appear. Since then postal officials have bestowed that honor on over seventy five important Black individuals, creating a colorful history of the Black experience in this country.

Do you know the issue dates of the following Black Heritage stamps?

1.

"Lift every voice and sing
'til earth and heaven ring,
Ring with the harmonies
of Liberty;
Let our rejoicing rise
High as the listening skies,
Let it resound loud as the
rolling sea."
—From "Lift Every Voice and Sing"
by *James Weldon Johnson*

2.

3.

ANSWERS ON PAGE 46

4.

5.

Martin Luther King Jr.

Black Heritage USA 15c

"I have a dream today…when we let freedom ring...we will be able To...join hands and sing...Free at Last! Free at last! Thank God Almighty, we are free at last!"
—*Martin Luther King, Jr.*

6.

Mary McLeod Bethune

Black Heritage USA 22

Answers on page 46

7. 

"Freedom is never given; it is won."
—*A. Philip Randolph*

8.

Jackie Robinson

Black Heritage USA 20c

9.

Carter G. Woodson

Black Heritage USA 20c

"He who teaches his race to hate another does not love his own."
—*Carter G. Woodson*

Answers on page 46

10. 

11. 

"This colored people going to be a people."
—*Sojourner Truth*

12. 

Answers on page 46

COMMON KNOWLEDGE

The following achievements and contributions all occurred in the same year. Can you identify the year?

1.
- Black candidates did well in elections. In Virginia, Douglas Wilder became the first elected Black governor in the United States history. In New York, David Dinkins was elected the city's first Black mayor. Coleman Young was re-elected to a fifth consecutive term as mayor of Detroit. Michael White was elected Mayor of Cleveland. Black mayors were also elected in Seattle, Washington; New Haven, Connecticut and Durham, North Carolina.

The year was: 1987 1988 1989

2.
- Shirley Ann Jackson was the first Black woman to chair the Nuclear Regulatory Commission.
- Floyd Adams, Jr., publisher of the Savannah Herald, a Black newspaper, was elected mayor of Savannah, Ga.
- Jesse Jackson, Jr., son of civil rights activist Rev. Jesse Jackson, is elected as the representative of Illinois's 2nd Congressional District.
- John Hope Franklin, received the first W.E.B. Dubois Award from the Fisk University Alumni Association.

The year was: 1994 1995 1996

3.
- President Clinton's Cabinet appointments included six Blacks; Clifton R. Wharton, Jr., Deputy Secretary of State Hazel R. O'Leary, Secretary of Energy; Mike Espy, Head of the Agriculture Department; Ron Brown, Secretary of Commerce; Jesse Brown, Veterans Affairs Secretary and Dr. Joycelyn Elders, Surgeon General.
- Alan Page, former pro football player, in the National football league, becomes the first Black American state supreme court justice in Minnesota.

The year was: 1992 1993 1994

ANSWERS ON PAGE 46

BLACK QUOTATIONS

1. "When you control a man's thinking you do not have to worry about his actions. You do not have to tell him not to stand here or go yonder. He will find his proper place and will stay in it. You do not need to send him to the back door. He will go without being told. In fact, if there is not back door, he will cut one for his special benefit." was said by who?
   a. Carter G. Woodson
   b. Benjamin Hooks
   c. James Baldwin
   d. Dick Gregory

2. "No two people on earth are alike and it's got to be that way in music or it isn't music." was said by who?
   a. Alice Walker
   b. Sojourner Truth
   c. Billie Holiday
   d. Josephine Baker

3. "Don't pray when it rains if you don't pray when the sun shines." was said by who?
   a. Dick Gregory
   b. Satchel Paige
   c. James Baldwin
   d. Ida B. Wells

4. "If you have no confidence in self, you are twice defeated in the race of life. With confidence you have won even before you have started." was said by who?

5. "Say it loud, I'm Black and I'm Proud." was said by who?
   a. Jesse Jackson
   b. Bob Gibson
   c. James Brown
   d. William Pickens

6. "I am my mother's daughter, and the drums of Africa still beat in my heart. They will not let me rest while there's a single Negro boy or girl without a chance to prove his worth". Was said by who?
   a. Maya Angelou
   b. Mary McLeod Bethune
   c. Alain Locke
   d. James Baldwin

7. "I am neither a Black politician nor a female politician, just a politician." Was said by who?
   a. Paul Robeson
   b. Barbara Jordan
   c. Jesse Jackson
   d. Ida B. Wells

ANSWERS ON PAGE 46

8. "Education is our passport to the future, for tomorrow belongs to the people who prepare for it today." was said by who?
   a. Malcolm X
   b. Richard Wright
   c. W.E.B. Du Bois
   d. W.C. Handy

9. "No person is your friend who demands your silence or denies your right to grow." was said by who?

10. "Would America have been America without her Negro people?" was said by who?
   a. Walter Mosley
   b. Billie Holiday
   c. W.E.B. Du Bois
   d. Jackie Robinson

11. "Winning as an American is very special, but winning as a Black American is a knockout!" was said by who?

12. "Ellis Island is for people who came over on ships. My people came in chains." was said by who?
   a. Maya Angelou
   b. James Baldwin
   c. Billie Holiday
   d. David Dinkins

13. "We didn't land on Plymouth Rock, Plymouth Rock landed on us." was said by who?

14. "My race and my gender have never been an issue for me, I have been blessed in knowing who I am and I am part of a great legacy." was said by who?
   a. Mae Jemison
   b. Billie Holiday
   c. Oprah Winfrey
   d. Maya Angelou

15. "Sometimes God has to get you alone by yourself so he can talk to your head." was said by who?

16. "I imagine one of the reason people cling to their hates so stubbornly is because they sense, once the hate is gone, they will be forced to deal with pain." was said by who?
   a. Langston Hughes
   b. James Baldwin
   c. Marcus Garvey
   d. Julian Bond

17. "I was free, but there was no one to welcome me to the land of freedom. I was a stranger in a strange land." was said by who?

Answers on page 46

Malcolm X

Did You Know

That Malcolm X (1925 - 1965) was born Malcolm Little in Omaha, Nebraska. While serving a prison term for burglary, Malcolm converted to Islam and changed his name to Malcolm X. In 1952, he began working with Elijah Muhammad and the Nation Of Islam (NOI). In March 1964, because of growing friction with Elijah Muhammad, Malcolm left the NOI. In the summer of 1964, he formed the Organization of Afro-American Unity (OAAU). On February 14, 1965, his house was fire-bombed, a week later, February 21, 1965, Malcolm X was shot to death as he gave a speech at the Audubon Ballroom in Harlem.

18. "When I was a child, my owner saw what he considered to be a good business deal and immediately accepted it. He traded me off for a horse." was said by who?
    a. George Washington Carver
    b. Harriet Tubman
    c. Booker T. Washington

19. "If a man can reach the latter days of his life with his soul intact, he has mastered life." was said by who?
    a. Gordon Parks
    b. Langston Hughes
    c. James Baldwin
    d. Paul Robeson

20. "You can't hold a man down without staying down with him." was said by who?
    a. James Baldwin
    b. Booker T. Washington
    c. Alice Walker

21. "There ain't nothing' an old man can do for me, but bring me a message from a young man." was said by who?

22. "Unconditional love not only means I am with you, but also I am for you, all the way, right or wrong." was said by who?
    a. Miles Davis
    b. James Baldwin
    c. Ray Charles
    d. Duke Ellington

23. "What happens to a dream deferred? Does it dry up like a raisin in the sun?" was said by who?
    a. Langston Hughes
    b. Billie Holiday
    c. Alice Walker
    d. Maya Angelou

24. "The test of what makes a Negro leader is not who shouts the loudest or gets the angriest but who gets the most results." was said by who?
    a. Jesse Jackson
    b. Dick Gregory
    c. Whitney M. Young, Jr.
    d. David Dinkins

25. "I refuse to let my nation's fixation with race and color deter me from fulfilling myself." was said by who?
    a. Bernard Shaw
    b. Harriet Tubman
    c. Toni Morrison

ANSWERS ON PAGE 46

BLACK FIRSTS

1. In 1946 the first coin , a fifty-cent piece honoring a Black American and designed by a Black American was issued. It became available on December 16, 1946, displaying the bust of who?
   a. Booker T. Washington
   b. Joe Louis
   c. Martin Luther King, Jr.
   d. W.C. Handy

2. In 1963, I was the first Black American graphic designer to design a U.S. postage stamp. The stamp was designed to commemorate the one-hundredth anniversary of the Emancipation Proclamation. Who Am I?
   a. George Herriman
   b. Isaac S. Hathaway
   c. George Olden
   d. E. Simms Campbell

3. In 1966, I became the first Black American showgirl with the Ringling Brothers Circus. Who Am I?
   a. Bernice Collins
   b. Janet Collins
   c. Toni Williams
   d. Katherine Dunham

4. In 1964, this Black American cartoonist and educator created "Wee Pals", the first integrated comic strip in the world. Influenced by Charles Schultz's "Peanuts" and inspired by Dick Gregory, "Wee Pals" became nationally syndicated and appeared in all of the large daily and Sunday comics. Who Am I?
   a. George Herriman
   b. Morris Turner
   c. George Olden
   d. E. Simms Campbell

5. I became the first Black American dancer in the country to become a member of a classical ballet company, the New York City Ballet. I founded the Dance Theater of Harlem, a school of dance for children regardless of race, it was the first Black classical ballet company in the United States and in 1988 headed the first Black cultural group to tour the Soviet Union. Who Am I?
   a. Arthur Mitchell
   b. Hemsley Winfield
   c. Alvin Ailey
   d. Buddy Bradley

6. In 1983, representing New York, I became the first Black American to be selected as Miss America in the 62 year history of the Atlantic

ANSWERS ON PAGE 46/47

City pageant. Who Am I?

a. Suzette Charles
b. Carole Gist
c. Vanessa Williams
d. Cheryl Adrenne Brown

7. In 1977, I became the first Black American to head a diocese in the Catholic Church in this century, when I became diocesan bishop of Biloxi, Mississippi. Who Am I?

a. Moses Anderson
b. Joseph Lawson Howze
c. Emerson J. Moore, Jr.
d. J. Terry Steib

8. On February 13, 1970, I became the first Black American member of the New York Stock Exchange. Who Am I?

a. Christine Bell
b. Jerome Holland
c. George Ellis Johnson
d. Joseph L. Searles III

9. A Black American businesswoman, philanthropist, and inventor, I was the first self made U.S. woman millionaire. I made my fortune in hair care products for Black women around the turn of the century. Who Am I?

10. On February 21, 1946, I became the first Black American to receive an honorary degree from Rollins College, a white college in Winter Park, Florida. Who Am I?

11. This university was established in 1915. It is the only historically Black Catholic university in North America. It is best known for its pre-med program, which is the first in the nation in placing Black American students in medical schools. The university is located in New Orleans, Louisiana. What is the name of the university?

12. On January 2, 1970, I became president of Michigan State University at East Lansing, the first Black American to preside over a predominantly white public. major American university in the twentieth century. I was named chancellor of the State University of New York in 1977. Who Am I?

a. Clifton R. Wharton, Jr.
b. Arthur Gary
c. James Colston
d. Harold L. Trigg

13. In 1950, I became the first Black American to be awarded the Nobel Peace Prize. The award was presented on September 22, 1950, for my peace efforts in the Middle East. In 1955, I was appointed Undersecretary for Special Political Affairs. Who Am I?

Answers on page 47

14. I was born in Los Angeles, California. I began my modeling career in Paris France in 1991. In 1997, I became the first Black American woman to appear on the cover of *Sports Illustrated* swimsuit issue. Who Am I?

15. I was the first Black American to head the Southern Sociological Society, also a distinguished sociologist. In 1921, I became director of research for the National Urban League in New York. I founded the League's magazine, *Opportunity*, in 1923. I became the first Black president of Fisk University in Nashville, Tennessee in 1946. Who Am I?
    a. Charles S. Johnson
    b. Alvin D. Loving, Sr.
    c. W. Montague Cobb
    d. Harold L. Trigg

16. In 1970, I became the first Black American to head the National Council of the Young Men's Christian Association (YMCA). In 1989, I was elected New Jersey's first Black Congressman. Who Am I?

17. On June 24, 1971, this brokerage firm was the first Black American company to become a member of the New York Stock Exchange. Name the two founders of the firm.

18. The first Black American daily newspaper in modern times began publishing on March 13, 1932. It was founded August 3, 1928 by William A. Scott III. In the spring of 1930, it became a bi-weekly. Name the newspaper?

19. I'm thought to be the first Black American woman to own and publish a newspaper in this country. In 1912, I bought the *Eagle*, and rename it the *California Eagle*, and ran it for some forty years. Who Am I?

20. The first issue of this magazine was published November 1, 1945 by Johnson Publishing Company, with John H. Johnson the company founder. The first issue sold 25,000 copies. What is the name of the magazine?

21. In 1980, I was appointed Washington correspondent and became the first Black American anchor at Cable News Network (CNN). My work has resulted in numerous awards, including an Emmy in 1989. Who Am I?

ANSWERS ON PAGE 47

22. I won the first Guggenheim fellowship awarded to a Black American photographer in 1952. Known for 40 years of photographs of the people of Harlem, I first studied architecture and sculpture at Cooper Union. My photos in *The Family of Men* toured the world in 1955. 1968 through 1975, I was a contract photographer for *Sport Illustrated.* Who Am I?
    a. Gordon A. Parks, Sr.
    b. Roy DeCarava
    c. Moneta J. Sleet, Jr.

23. In 1961, I made history by being the first Black student, along with Hamilton Homes to integrate the University of Georgia. In 1978, I became the first Black American woman to anchor a national newscast, The MacNeil Lehrer Report. In 1999, I joined CNN in Johannesburg, South Africa, as bureau chief. Who Am I?
    a. Charlayne Hunter-Gault
    b. Jewel Limar Prestage
    c. Bettye J. Davis

24. In 1951, I was named pastor of Zion Baptist Church in Philadelphia. In 1964, I founded The Opportunities Industrialization Center (OIC), which provided job training for Black American men and women. In 1971, I became the first Black American to serve on the board of directors of General Motors. Who Am I?
    a. Jerome Holland
    b. Leon H. Sullivan
    c. Adam Clayton Powell

25. In 1955, I became the first Black American woman president of Bennett College in Greensboro, North Carolina. I was also the first Black woman in the United States to be named president of a four year women's college. Who Am I?
    a. Mary E. Branch
    b. Mary McLeod Bethune
    c. Willa B. Player

ANSWERS ON PAGE 47

MILESTONES

1. April 3, 1944, the Supreme Court rules in *Smith v. Allwright*, that white primaries cannot deny Black American citizens their right to vote in state primary elections.

2. November 1, 1951 marks the publication of the first issue of *Jet* magazine by Johnson Publishing Company. The magazine offers weekly news coverage of Black American.

3. March 15, 1933, the NAACP files its first lawsuit, against the University of North Carolina, in its effort to stop discrimination in public schools.

4. January 11, 1957, the Southern Christian Leadership Conference (SCLC) is founded.

5. August 18, 1963, James Meredith graduates from the University of Mississippi.

6. January 3, 1964, Martin Luther King appears on the cover of *Time* magazine as "Man of The Year".

7. August 1, 1914, in Jamaica Marcus Garvey founds the Universal Negro Improvement Association.

8. 1909, Dr. William A. Attaway founded the Mississippi Life Insurance Company, the first Black American legal reserve life insurance company.

9. In 1949, Jesse Blanton, Sr. founded the first Black American owned radio station. It was WERD-am in Atlanta, Georgia.

10. March 19, 1982 Clarence Pendleton became the first Black American to be confirmed by the U.S. Senate to head the U.S. Civil Rights Commission.

Black American Landmarks

1. This two-story frame house belonging to the Black American activist and educator Mary McLeod Bethune was built in 1920 on the campus of the school she established in 1904. The house was proclaimed a National Historic Landmark when? Month, date and year.

2. In 1874 Blanche K. Bruce was elected United States senator from Mississippi, becoming the second Black American to hold the position and the first to serve a full term. Perhaps his most significant accomplishment was handing the affairs of the Freemen's Savings Bank after its collapse in 1874. Through Bruce's efforts, investors were able to recover three-fifths of the money they had deposited in the failed bank. Blanche K. Bruce's Washington residence was designated a National Historic Landmark when? Month, date and year.

3. Founded in 1881 by Booker Taliaferro Washington, Tuskegee Institute, now Tuskegee University became a major force in launching Black Americans into higher education. Tuskegee Institute was established by an act of the General Assembly of Alabama on February 12, 1881, and Booker T. Washington as its founder and first principal opened the school on July of that year. Between 1881 and 1915 Washington put into practice a program of industrial and vocational education for Black Americans. Tuskegee Institute was designated a National Historic Landmark when? Month, date and year.

4. Carter G. Woodson was born the son of former slaves on December 19, 1875, in New Canton, Virginia. Woodson earn his Ph.D. from Harvard University in 1912. He was the second Black American to receive a doctorate from Harvard, W.E.B. DuBois was the first. In 1915 he organized the Association for the Study of Negro Life and History. Woodson died on April 3, 1950. When was the Woodson House designated a National Historic Landmark? Month, date and year.

5. In 1903, Maggie Lean Walker founded the successful bank, Saint Luke Penny Savings Bank,—which became the St. Luke Bank and Trust Company—to became the first Black American woman to establish and head a bank. In addition to being the first Black woman

 Answers on page 47

Justina Ford House

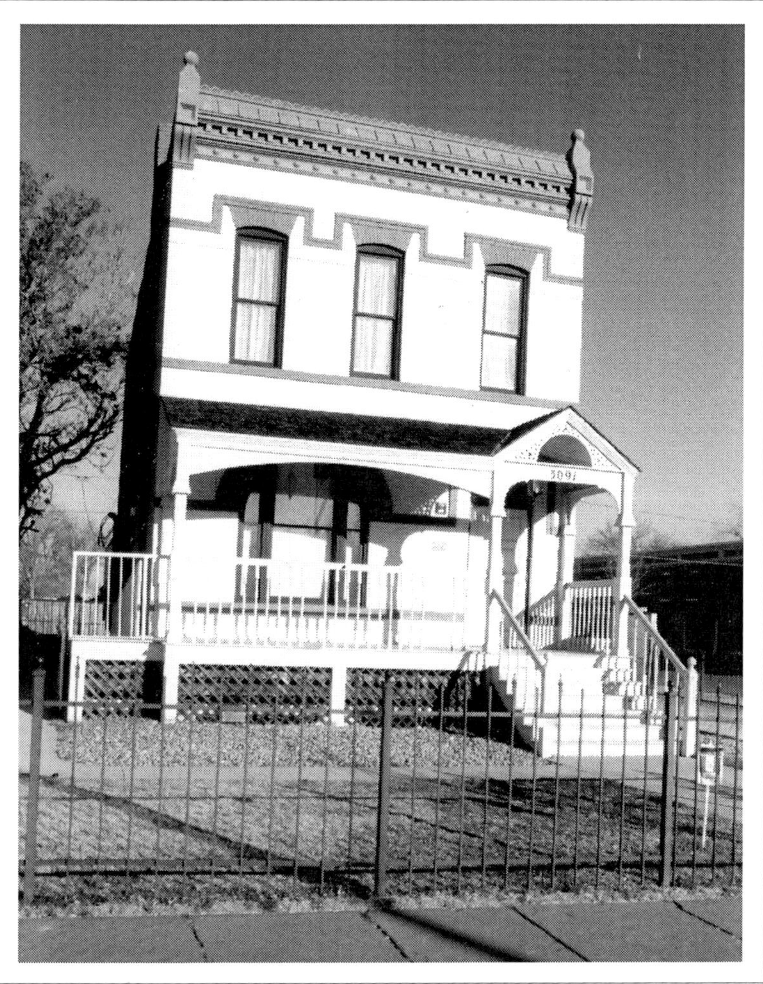

Did You Know

That Justina Ford was the first Black American woman physician in Denver, Colorado. Following her graduation in 1899 from Hering Medical School in Chicago, IL, Ford directed a hospital in Normal, Alabama for two years. She moved to Denver in 1902, specializing in pediatrics, gynecology and obstetrics, she became known as the "baby doctor", delivering over 7,000 babies. Justina Ford's home and office was relocated, renovated and reopened as the Black American West Museum located in Denver, Colorado.

Melvin F. Luster House

Did You Know

That Melvin F. Luster's House was built by Sydney Lyons, a highly successful Black American businessman and his wife. Lyons established the East India Toilet Goods Company. In 1909, Lyons moved to Oklahoma City and sold toiletries, he also owned and operated a grocery store. Lyons products were sold nationally and in many foreign countries. Few Black Americans in Oklahoma City were as successful in business as Lyons in the early 20th century.

president of a bank, she was editor of a newspaper which was considered to be one of the best papers in America. In 1912, she organized the Richmond Council of Black Women, which raised money to establish a school and farm for the training of delinquent Black girls. Despite an illness that confined her to a wheelchair, she chaired the board of directors of the St. Luke Penny Savings Bank until her death. The Richmond home in which she lived from 1909 until her death on December 15, 1934, was designated a National Historic Landmark when? Month, date and year.

6. Oakland Chapel on Alcorn Campus was built in 1838. It's the oldest building on Alcorn University's Campus. The chapel symbolizes the importance of Alcorn as the first Black land grant college in the United States. When was Oakland Chapel designated a National Historic Landmark when? Month, date and year.

7. During the years between 1900 and 1903, when Scott Joplin lived in an apartment complex on Delmar Boulevard, in St. Louis, Missouri, were some of the most creative and important years of Joplin musical career. Some of the music he composed during this time includes "*Peacherine Rag*", "*Little Black Baby*", and "*The Entertainer.*" This residence is the only building still in existence in the United States that can be positively linked to Scott Joplin. Scott Joplin died in 1917, in New York City. When was Joplin's St. Louis residence designated a National Historic Landmark? Month, date and year.

8. In 1947, Jackie Robinson became the first Black American to play in the major leagues. When he signed his baseball contract, he broke the color barrier against Black American's participation in professional sports. While playing for the Brooklyn Dodgers, he lived in the Borough of New York City for many years. When was the residence of Jackie Robinson designated a National Historic Landmark? Month, date and year.

9. From 1941 to 1947, this was the residence of a Black American poet and writer who was often called the father of the Harlem Renaissance. He is known for such works as *If We Must Die*; his autobiography, *A Long Way From Home* and the first book by a Black American to reach the best seller list, *Home To Harlem*. He was born in Jamaica, British West Indies. He died penniless in 1948, at age 58. On December 8, 1976, his New York residence was designated a National Historic Landmark. Name the residence.

ANSWERS ON PAGE 47

Blacks In Military

1. I was promoted to the rank of brigadier general in 1940, becoming the first Black American to hold this position in the United States Army. Who Am I?

2. In 1945, I became the first Black American nurse commissioned in the Navy Reserve Corps. A registered nurse from New York City, I was sworn in as an ensign. Who Am I?

3. In January 1962, I was given command of the destroyer USS *Falgout.* A veteran of three wars, in 1971, I became the first Black American admiral in United States history. Who Am I?

4. In 1952, I became the first Black American Marine pilot and in 1979, the first Black general in the United States Marines. Who Am I?

5. In 1975, I became the nation's first Black American four-star general in the United States Air Force. I was also named commander of the North American Air Defense Command (NORAD) in Colorado. Who Am I?

6. In 1989, I became the first Black American to serve as chairman of the Joint Chiefs of Staff and principal military advisor to the President of the United States, the Secretary of Defense, and the National Security Council. Who Am I?

7. In 1977, I became the First Black American to be appointed Secretary of the Army. Who Am I?

8. I became the first Black American pilot in the United States Naval Reserve in 1949. On December 4, 1950, at Changjin Reservoir in Korea, I became the first Black American naval pilot killed in action. Who Am I?

9. The Congressional Medal of Honor is awarded to private William Thompson of Brooklyn, who was killed in combat during the Korean War. He was the first Black American to receive this award since the Spanish-American War. What was the year?

Answers on page 47

General Benjamin O. Davis, Jr.

Did You Know

That Benjamin O. Davis, Jr. was the first Black American general in the United States Air Force. In July 1932, Davis entered the United States Military Academy at West Point. At West Point, he was subjected to a deplorable four year campaign called "silencing", by his fellow cadets, a form of punishing a classmate for having committed some infraction. In Davis' case the infraction was being Black. Fifty years would pass before Davis would return to West Point. General Davis' service career spanned World War II, Korea and Vietnam. He commanded the 51st Fighter Interceptor Squadron in Korea and flew the F-86 in the Korean War. He commanded the 13th Air Force from 1967 to 1968, in the Vietnam War. Davis retired as a Lieutenant General in 1979 and was advanced to four star General in 1998 by President Bill Clinton. Davis died on July 4, 2002.

Admiral J. Paul Reason

Did You Know

That Admiral J. Paul Reason, is the Navy's first Black American four star Admiral. His naval service began after graduating from Naval Academy in 1965. In 1970, he earned a master's degree in the management of computer systems. Upon promotion to Four-Star Admiral, Reason assumed duties as Commander in Chief, United States Atlantic Fleet in December 1996. Some of Admiral Reason's awards include the Distinguished Service Medal, Legion of Merit, Republic of Vietnam Honor Medal, Republic of Vietnam Campaign Medal and Navy Commendation Medal.

10. In 1961, I became the first Black American sentry appointed to guard the Tomb of The Unknown Soldier. Who Am I?
    a. Fred Moore
    b. Osborne E. Scott
    c. Alford McMichael

11. The USS *Jesse L. Brown* is launched from Louisiana. It is the first United States Navy ship named for a Black American officer. Brown was killed in action during the Korean War. What was the year that the ship was launched?
    a. 1999
    b. 1972
    c. 1964

12. A graduate of the University of Wisconsin and the Army ROTC program in 1979, I earn my aviator wings and became the first Black American woman pilot in the United States armed services history. Who Am I?
    a. Marcella A. Hayes
    b. Hazel W. Johnson
    c. Phyllis Mae Daley

13. In September 1990, I was promoted to brigadier general and became vice commander Air Logistics Center at Tinker Air Force Base in Midwest City Oklahoma. In 1993, I was assigned to Randolph Air Force Base in Texas, as director of technical training, air education and teaming command. Who Am I?

14. In May 1960, I was commissioned as a first lieutenant in the United States Army Nurse Corps. In 1979, at the age of fifty two, I was promoted to brigadier general, the first Black American woman general in the United States military history. Who Am I?

15. I became the first Black American woman to attend the United States Naval Academy and in 1980, I became the academy's first Black American woman to graduate. Who Am I?
    a. Janie L. Mines
    b. Hazel W. Johnson
    c. Marcella A. Hayes

Answers on page 47

Answer Key

History

1. Reginald Lewis
2. Montgomery Bus Boycott
3. NAACP
4. Dave Bing
5. Matthew Alexander Henson
6. Jean Blackwell Hutson
7. Asa Philip Randolph
8. Ed Bradley
9. Essence
10. Joseph Echols Lowery
11. October 25, 1997
12. Robert Sengstacke Abbott
13. Carter Godwin Woodson
14. Bessie Coleman
15. Kenneth Bancroft Clark
16. October 16, 1995
17. George Washington Carver
18. Rosa Parks
19. b. John Hope Franklin
20. a. Martin Luther King, Jr.
21. c. Alain Leroy Locke
22. United Negro College Fund
23. Fisk University
24. b. Tom Joyner
25. b. Franklin A. Thomas

Black Heritage Stamps

1. February 2, 1988
2. February 1, 1978
3. June 9, 1983
4. January 30, 1981
5. January 13, 1979
6. March 5, 1985
7. February 3, 1989
8. August 2, 1982
9. February 1, 1984
10. February 15, 1980
11. February 4, 1986
12. February 20, 1987

Common Knowledge

1. 1989
2. 1995
3. 1993

Black Quotations

1. a. Carter G. Woodson
2. c. Billie Holiday
3. b. Satchel Paige
4. Marcus Garvey
5. c. James Brown
6. a. Maya Angelou
7. b. Barbara Jordan
8. a. Malcolm X
9. Alice Walker
10. c. W.E.B. Du Bois
11. Toni Morrison
12. d. David Dinkins
13. Malcolm X
14. c. Oprah Winfrey
15. T.D. Jakes
16. b. James Baldwin
17. Harriet Tubman
18. a. George Washington Carver
19. a. Gordon Parks
20. b. Booker T. Washington
21. Jackie "Moms" Mabley
22. d. Duke Ellington
23. a. Langston Hughes
24. c. Whitney M. Young, Jr.
25. a. Bernard Shaw

Black Firsts

1. a. Booker T. Washington

Black Firsts

2. c. George Olden
3. c. Toni Williams
4. b. Morris Turner
5. a. Arthur Mitchell
6. c. Vanessa Williams
7. b. Joseph Lawson Howze
8. d. Joseph L. Searles III
9. Madame C.J. Walker
10. Mary McLeod Bethume
11. Xavier University
12. a. Clifton R. Wharton, Jr.
13. Ralph Bunche
14. Tyra Banks
15. a. Charles S. Johnson
16. Donald M. Payne
17. Willie L. Daniels/Travers Bell, Jr.
18. Atlanta Daily World
19. Charlotta Spears Bass
20. Ebony
21. Bernard Shaw
22. b. Roy DeCarava
23. a. Charlayne Hunter-Gault
24. b. Leon H. Sullivan
25. c. Willa B. Player

Black American Landmarks

1. December 2, 1974
2. May 15, 1976
3. June 23, 1965
4. May 11, 1976
5. May 12, 1975
6. May 11, 1976
7. December 8, 1976
8. May 11, 1976
9. Claude McKay Residence

Blacks In Military

1. Benjamin O. Davis, Sr.
2. Phyllis Mae Daley
3. Samuel Lee Gravely, Jr.
4. Frank E. Peterson, Jr.
5. General Daniel H. James, Jr.
6. General Colin L. Powell
7. Clifford Alexander, Jr.
8. Jesse Leroy Brown
9. 1951
10. a. Fred Moore
11. b. 1972
12. a. Marcella A. Hayes
13. General Marcelite J. Harris
14. Hazel W. Johnson
15. a. Janie L. Mines

Civil Rights & Political Leaders

Black Mayors

1. On November 7, 1967, I became the first Black mayor of Cleveland, Ohio. Who Am I?

2. September, 1967, President Lyndon Johnson reorganized the government of the District of Columbia and appointed me the first mayor of Washington, DC. Seven years later, (1974), the residents of the District of Columbia were given the right to elect their own mayor, they elected me, making me the first Black elected mayor of the nation's capital. Who Am I?

3. May 29, 1973, I became the first Black American to be elected mayor of Los Angeles, California. I served for 20 years, longer than any previous mayor of Los Angeles. Who Am I?

4. November 6, 1973, I became the first Black American mayor of Detroit, Michigan. Who Am I?

5. October 16, 1973, Maynard Jackson was elected mayor of this city, becoming the first Black American mayor in the South. Name the city.

6. November 7, 1967, I became the first Black American mayor of Gary Indiana. Who Am I?

7. I was the first Black American to become United States Ambassador to the United Nations. In 1982, I was elected mayor of Atlanta, Georgia. Who Am I?

8. In 1980, I won the election to the United States House of Representatives. In 1983, I was elected Chicago's first Black American mayor. I was re-elected in 1987, but died of a massive heart attack on November 25, Who Am I?

9. September 11, 1990, Sharon Pratt Kelly was elected mayor of this city, becoming the first Black American woman to lead a major American city. Name the city?

Answers on page 70

Andrew Young

Did You Know

That Andrew Young was the first Black American United States Ambassador to the United Nations. Young began his political career working with Martin Luther King, Jr. in the Civil Rights Movement of the early 1960s. Young became executive director of the Southern Christian Leadership Conference in 1964, and executive vice president in 1967. In 1982, Young became mayor of Atlanta, he serve for eight years.

10. I was the first Black American to become mayor of Denver, Colorado. I took office on June 30, 1991. Who Am I?

11. May 13, 1969, I became the first Black American to be elected mayor of Fayette, Mississippi. Who Am I?

12. On January 2, 1984, I became the first Black American to be elected mayor of Philadelphia. Who Am I?

13. On November 7, 1989, I became the first Black American to be elected mayor of New York City. Who Am I?

14. On October 30, 1979, Richard Arrington, Jr. became the first Black American to be elected mayor of what city?

15. On October 28, 1981, Edward M. McIntyre, a graduate of Morehouse College, became the first Black American to be elected mayor of this city. Name the city.
    a. Atlanta, GA
    b. Savannah, GA
    c. Augusta, GA
    d. Houston, TX

16. Will W. Herenton became the first Black American to be elected mayor of this city. He was also the first Black superintendent of this city's school system. Name the city.
    a. Memphis, TN
    b. Richmond, VA
    c. Dallas, TX
    d. Nashville, TN

17. On April 16, 1973, Lelia Smith Foly, was elected the first Black woman mayor in the United States when she became mayor of this small all-Black town of about 500. What is the name of the town?
    a. Taft, OK
    b. St. Louis, MO
    c. Fayette, MS
    d. Kansas City, MO

18. On June 16, 1970, Kenneth Allen Gibson was elected the first Black mayor of a major Eastern city, taking office on July 1. He was also the first Black president of the U.S. Conference of Mayors, in July 1976. Name the city.
    a. Newark, NJ
    b. New York City, NY
    c. Buffalo, NY
    d. Oakland, CA

19. On April 6, 1971, I became the first Black American to be elected mayor of East St. Louis. Who Am I?

ANSWERS ON PAGE 70

20. In 1992, I became the first Black popularly elected mayor of Cincinnati, OH. The two Black mayors who had held that office previously had been chosen by the city council. Who Am I?
   a. Dwight Tillery
   b. Robert Clayton Henry
   c. Carl Stokes
   d. Theodore Barry

21. In 1969, I was elected mayor of Chapel Hill, North Carolina becoming the first Black American to be elected mayor in a predominantly white Southern city. Who Am I?
   a. Andrew Young
   b. Richard Hatcher
   c. Howard N. Lee

22. In 1983, I became the first Black American to be elected mayor of Charlotte, North Carolina. I held the office for two terms, from 1983 to 1987. Who Am I?
   a. Harvey Bernard Gantt
   b. Charles Evers
   c. Coleman Young

23. In 1972, I became the first Black American to be appointed mayor of Cincinnati, OH. I was chosen by the city council, rather than by popular vote. Who Am I?
   a. Theodore Moody Berry
   b. Dwight Tillery
   c. George James
   d. Perry B. Jackson

24. In 1984, I became the first Black mayor of Union Springs, Alabama. The same election day also saw Mary Stoval , of Hurtsboro and Nathanial Torian of Hillsboro elected first Black mayors of their towns. Who Am I?
   a. John McGowan
   b. Carl Stokes
   c. Andrew Young

25. As mayor of Mount Vernon, NY in 1985, I became the first Black American to be elected mayor in the state of New York. Who Am I?
   a. David Dinkins
   b. Ronald A. Blackwood
   c. Coleman Young

Answers on page 70

Ronald V. Dellums

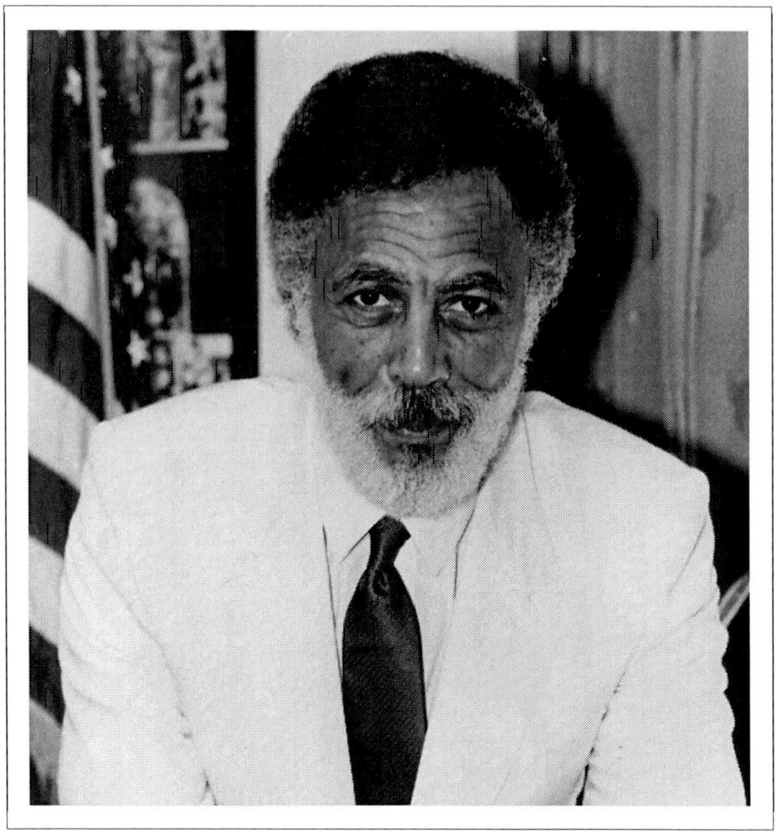

Did You Know

That Ronald Dellums was elected to the United States House of Representatives in 1970, a Representative from California's Ninth District. He was the first Black American to chair the House Armed Services Committee. Dellums was also chairman of the Congressional Black Caucus. Congressman Dellums retired in February 1998, after 27 years of service in the House of Representatives.

Milestones

1. January 10, 1925 Adelvert H. Roberts was elected to the Illinois state legislature, the first Black American to serve in a state assembly in at least twenty-five years.

2. August 1, 1944 Adam Clayton Powell, Jr. one of the most controversial politicians of the twentieth century, was elected United States Congressman from Harlem, becoming the first Black American member of the House of Representatives from the East.

3. August 28, 1963 the largest single protest demonstration in the United States history occurred at the Lincoln Memorial in Washington, DC, where over 250,000 Black and White Americans gathered to lobby for passage of sweeping Civil Rights measures by congress. Martin Luther King, Jr. thrilled the crowd with his immortal *"I Have a Dream"* speech.

4. On December 10, 1964 Martin Luther King, Jr. was awarded the Nobel Peace Prize in Oslo, Norway. At age thirty-five, King became the youngest man in history and the second Black American to receive this prestigious award.

5. On January 25, 1966 Constance Baker Motley was appointed a federal judge by President Lyndon B. Johnson. She was the second Black woman to hold such a post.

6. June, 1970 Charles Rangel, a Black Harlem politician, defeated incumbent Adam Clayton Powell, Jr. for his long held seat in the U.S. House of Representatives. Eight Black Americans sat in the House during 1970; William L. Dawson, Charles C. Diggs, Jr., Louis Stokes, Augustus F. Hawkins, John Conyers, Shirley Chisholm and Robert C. Nix.

7. 1979, Audrey Neal became the first Black American and woman of any ethnic group to work as a longshoreman on the U.S. Eastern seaboard.

8. 1978, the first stamp of the United States Postal Service's Black Heritage Series, honors Harriet Tubman.

9. May 1, 1946 former Federal Judge William H. Hastie was confirmed as governor of the Virgin Islands. Hastie became the only Black American to govern a United States, state or territory since Reconstruction.

10. January 13, 1990 Lawrence Douglas Wilder was inaugurated as governor of Virginia, making him the first Black American to be elected chief executive of a state in America's history.

11. In 1905, Charles W. Anderson became the first Black American appointed by a president to hold office north of the Mason Dixon line. He was appointed Collector of Internal Revenue for the Second District of New York.

12. Jesse Ernest Wilkins, Sr. was the first Black American, assistant secretary of labor. He was appointed on March 4, 1954, by President Dwight D. Eisenhower.

13. In 1961, Robert C. Weaver was named administrator of the Housing and Home Finance Agency, making him the highest ranking Black in the Federal government at that time.

14. In 1972, Robert Wedgeworth, Jr. was named director of the American Library Association, the first Black American to hold this position.

15. In 1929, Oscar Stanton DePriest became the first Black congressman elected in the twentieth century and also the first Black American to be elected from a northern state.

Edward W. Brooke

Did You Know

That Edward W. Brooke, III was a Senator from Massachusetts. He was the first Black American ever to be elected to the Senate by popular vote since Reconstruction. Brooke was appointed chairman of the Boston Finance Commission in 1961. In 1962, he was elected attorney general of the Commonwealth of Massachusetts, reelected in 1964, and was elected a Republican to the United States Senate in 1966.

BLACK FIRSTS

1. Democratic member of the United States House of Representatives, I am the first Black American woman to be elected to the House of Representatives from the state of Georgia. Who Am I?
   a. Cynthia McKinney
   b. Sheila Jackson-Lee
   c. Diane Abbott
   d. Maxine Moore Waters

2. On June 11, 1987, I made history by becoming the first Black female member of the British Parliament. Who Am I?
   a. Barbara Lee
   b. Carrie Meek
   c. Diane Abbott
   d. Carol Moseley-Braun

3. I was sworn into the 103rd congress on January 3, 1993. I was one of six women who served in the United States Senate during that session, and the first Black American woman to serve as a United States Senator. Who Am I?
   a. Shirley Chisholm
   b. Carol Moseley-Braum
   c. Carrie Meek
   d. Barbara Jordan

4. I was the first Black American to serve as chairman of a national political party. I was also the first Black chief counsel of a senate standing committee and the first Black law partner at Patton, Boggs, and Blow. In 1993, President Bill Clinton appointed me Secretary of Commerce, making me the first Black American to hold that position. My self, and 34 others were on a three-day economic tour of the Balkans for the Department of Commerce when our plane crashed during stormy weather. Who Am I?

5. I served my home state of Virginia as state senator, lieutenant governor, and the First Black American to be elected governor in the United States. Who Am I?
   a. Lawrence Douglas Wilder
   b. Carl Stokes
   c. P.B. S. Pinchback
   d. Harold Washington

6. On January 18, 1966, I became the first Housing and Urban Development (HUD) Secretary, and the first Black American Cabinet member to be sworn in. Who Am I?

ANSWERS ON PAGE 70

Colin L. Powell

Did You Know

That Colin Luther Powell (April 5, 1937), became a four-star general and served as the 12th Chairman of the Joint Chiefs of Staff, Department of Defense, from October 1, 1989 to September 30, 1993, under both President George H. Bush and President Bill Clinton, becoming the first Black American and the youngest person to chair the Joint Chiefs of Staff. He served two tours of duty in Vietnam, and as a battalion commander in Korea. In September of 1993, Powell retired from the military.

7. I was the first Black American woman elected to the United States House of Representatives in 1968. In 1972, I became the first Black woman to seek nomination as the Democrats' presidential candidate. Who Am I?

   a. Shirley Chisholm
   b. Carrie Meek
   c. Barbara Jordan
   d. Carol Moseley-Braun

8. In 1977, I was appointed U.S. Secretary of Housing and Urban Development by President Jimmy Carter, becoming the first Black American woman to serve in this position as well as in a Cabinet level position. I was appointed secretary of the Department of Health, Education, and Welfare in 1979. My tenure was cut short by the election of Ronal Reagan in 1980. Who Am I?

9. I became the first Black American to be appointed to the federal bench in 1937, I was appointed United States district judge in the Virgin Islands. I was also the first Black governor of the Virgin Islands in 1946, and became judge of the circuit court of appeals in 1949. Who Am I?

10. In 1945, I became the first Black American judge of a United States court. This was the first time that a Black American served as a federal judge in the United States. I was educated at the University of Chicago and Oberlin College. Who Am I?

11. Journalist and political activist, I was the first Black American woman to run for vice president in 1952. I was the nominee of the Progressive Party. Who Am I?

12. November 8, 1966 I became the first Black American to be elected to the United States Senate since Reconstruction, and the first ever to be elected by popular vote. Who Am I?

    a. Edward W. Brooke, III
    b. John Conyers
    c. Adam Clayton Powell
    d. Charles Rangel

13. I was elected congresswoman from Illinois, to complete my husband's unexpired term. I took office in 1973, becoming the first Black American to serve in the Congress. In 1975, I became the first Black American and the first woman to chair the Manpower and Housing Subcommittee of the House Government Operations Committee, and the first Black woman to chair the Congressional Black Congress. Who Am I?

ANSWERS ON PAGE 70

Thurgood Marshall

Did You Know

That Thurgood Marshall (July 2, 1908 - January 24, 1993), was the first Black American U.S. Supreme Court Justice, founder of the NAACP's Legal Defense and Educational Fund, lawyer whose victory in Brown v. Board of Education (1954) outlawed segregation in American public schools. When Marshall died in 1993, he was only the second Justice to lie in State in the Supreme Court's Chambers. Marshall brought 32 cases before the Supreme Court, he won 29 of them. He had an even more impressive record as a judge for the U.S. Court of Appeals, a position to which President John F. Kennedy appointed him in 1961. Of the 112 opinions he wrote for that court, not one was overturned on appeal.

14. Lawyer, public official, football player and coach, I was the first Black American to be appointed to a sub-cabinet post. President William Howard Taft appointed me assistant attorney general of the United States on November 26, 1911. Who Am I?

15. I was elected to the Pennsylvania House of Representatives in 1938, the first time a Black American woman had been elected to a state legislature. Who Am I?

16. In 1939, I became the first Black American woman judge in the United States, when I was appointed to the Domestic Relations Court of New York City. Who Am I?
    a. Jane M. Bolin
    b. Diane Abbott
    c. Crystal Byrd Fauset

17. In 1927, I became the first woman to receive a master of law degree from Loyola University. In 1950, I was appointed an alternate delegate to the United Nations by President Harry Truman, becoming the first Black American to represent the United States at the United Nations. In 1962, I became the first Black woman to be elected judge to the municipal court of Chicago. Who Am I?
    a. Clara Williams
    b. Cynthia McKinney
    c. Edith Sampson

18. I was drawn into Civil Rights while selling insurance in the Mississippi Delta region. In 1954, I became the NAACP field secretary for Mississippi. On June 12, 1963, I was shot to death in the driveway of my home. Who Am I?
    a. Medgar Evers
    b. Martin Luther King, Jr.
    c. William Henry Hastie

19. In 1961, I became the first Black American to be appointed judge of a United States district court in the United States. In 1975, I became the first Black American to serve as chief of a United States district court. Who Am I?
    a. Clarence Thomas
    b. James Benton Parsons
    c. Robert C. Weaver

ANSWERS ON PAGE 70

20. In 1976, I became the first Black American to call the roll at the Republican Party National Convention, which was held in Detroit, Michigan. Who Am I?

21. In 1970, I became the first Black American to be elected to represent Missouri in Congress. Who Am I?
    a. William H. Lewis
    b. William L. Clay
    c. Vernon E. Jordan

22. Educated at Morgan State and Johns Hopkins, I was elected to Congress from Maryland's 7th District in 1987. I served on the House Commission on Banking, Finance, and Urban Affairs, and on the Joint Economic Commission. On February 20, 1996, I left Congress to become president and CEO of the NAACP. Who Am I?
    a. Kweisi Mfume
    b. Robert C. Weaver
    c. Andrew Young

23. In 1972, I was elected to the United States House of Representatives, from Texas. I became the first Black American woman from the South to serve in congress. Who Am I?
    a. Barbara Jordan
    b. Shirley Chisholm
    c. Carol Moseley-Braun

24. I served as field director for the Georgia branch of the NAACP from 1961 to 1963. In 1970, I became executive director of the United Negro College Fund. From 1992 to 1993, I was chair of President-elect Bill Clinton's transition team. Who Am I?
    a. Kweisi Mfume
    b. Vernon E. Jordan
    c. John Conyers

25. I became the first Black American woman admitted to the Illinois bar in 1920. On January 29, 1926, I became the first Black woman lawyer admitted to practice before the United States Supreme Court. Who Am I?
    a. Mary Terrell
    b. Eleanor Norton
    c. Violette N. Anderson

Answers on page 70

Shirley Chisholm

Did You Know

That Shirley Chisholm was the first Black American woman to be elected to the United States House of Representatives. She was elected to Congress from New York's Twelfth District. In 1972, Chisholm became the first Black American to make a bid for the presidential nomination of the Democratic party.

Who's Who

1. In 1965, I won a seat in the Georgia House of Representatives in a newly created Black district in Atlanta. Statements that I made against the war in Vietnam led the House to bar me from my seat. In December 1966, the Supreme Court ruled in my favor and I was seated in 1967. In 1998, I was elected chairman of the National Association for the Advancement of Colored People (NAACP). Who Am I?

   a. Julian Bond　　c. Maynard Jackson
   b. John Lewis　　d. Earl Hilliard

2. Minister and Civil Rights leader, in 1957, I helped Martin Luther King, Jr. found the Southern Christian Leadership Council (SCLC) to coordinate nonviolent resistance to segregation. After King's assassination in 1968, I became SCLC president until I resigned in 1977. Who Am I?

3. Black American minister, founder of Operation Push and the National Rainbow Coalition, and twice a candidate for president of the United States. Who Am I?

   a. Jesse Louis Jackson, Sr.　　c. Julian Bond
   b. William Gray　　d. Benjamin Hooks

4. I was elected to congress in 1978, I served on the Democratic Congressional Steering Committee, the Congressional Black Caucus, the House Foreign Affairs Committee, and the Budget Committee. I was the first Black American to chair the House Budget Committee. In 1989, I became the first Black American to serve as a majority whip in the House. I gave up my congressional career in 1991, to head the United Negro College Fund (UNCF). Who Am I?

5. After the assassination of my husband in 1968, I continued to lead major demonstrations in support of striking workers and the poor, organized marches to promote my husband principles, such as the 20th Anniversary March on Washington in 1983. In 1986, I prevailed in my campaign to establish a national holiday honoring my late husband. Who Am I?

Answers on page 70

6. Four time mayor of Washington, D.C. and founding member of the Student Nonviolent Coordinating Committee (SNCC), my election to a fourth term as mayor of Washington, D.C. came three years after a conviction for cocaine possession. I received my bachelor's degree in chemistry in 1958, and did my postgraduate study at Fisk University in Nashville, where I organized the campus's first National Association for the Advancement of Colored People (NAACP) chapter. Who Am I?

7. In 1955, I was appointed to serve as the National Association for the Advancement of Colored People (NAACP) Executive Director, the organization's highest administrative post. I steered the NAACP through the Civil Rights Movement's most turbulent era, and with Martin Luther King, Jr. helped to organize the March on Washington in 1963. Who Am I?
   a. Medgar Evers
   b. Roy Ottoway Wilkins
   c. Robert C. Weaver

8. I served as the executive director of the National Association for the Advancement of Colored People (NAACP) from April 1993 to August 1994. I helped organize the 1995, Million Man March. Who Am I?

9. I began my civil rights activities in Washington D.C., where my husband was a municipal judge. In 1901, I joined W.E.B. Du Bois as a founding member of the National Association for the Advancement of Colored People (NAACP) and served as head of the Washington chapter. I have written numerous magazine articles, and in 1940, an autobiography, *A Colored Woman in a White World.* Who Am I?
   a. Mary Terrell
   b. Coretta Scott King
   c. Cardiss Collins

10. During the 1920s and 30s, I headed the Alabama branch of the Brotherhood of Sleeping Car Porters. I served as president of the NAACP's Montgomery branch from 1939 to 1951. I was instrumental in organizing the Montgomery Bus Boycott. My achievement earned me the nickname "Mr. Civil Rights" Who Am I?
   a. Robert C. Weaver
   b. Edgar Daniel Nixon
   c. Julian Bond

ANSWERS ON PAGE 70

Common Knowledge

The following achievements and/or events all occurred in the same year. Can you identify the year?

1.

- Marian Wright Edelman, children's rights activist and a lawyer, founded the Children's Defense Fund.
- September 17, the state of Illinois becomes the first state to pass legislation honoring Martin Luther King, Jr. with a state holiday.
- Maynard H. Jackson is elected the first Black American mayor of Atlanta.
- August 15, Eleanor Holmes Norton helps found the National Black Feninist Organization.

The year was: 1973 1974 1975

2.

- The United States Congress passes the Civil Rights Acts of 19 , prohibiting discrimination in public accommodations, employment, and education.
- Three civil rights workers, James Earl Chaney, Andrew Goodman, and Michael Schwerner are murdered in Mississippi.
- Carl Thomas Rowan became the first Black American to attend a meeting of the National Security Council.

The year was: 1963 1964 1965

3.

- Martin Luther King, Jr. leads the Selma-to-Montgomery March in Alabama.
- May 30, Vivian Malone graduated from the University of Alabama, becoming the first Black American to graduate from this predominantly white university.
- The Voting Rights Act of 19 , is signed by President Johnson.
- James Madison Nabrit, Jr. becomes the first Black American ambassador to the United Nations.

The year was: 1965 1968 1969

Answers on page 70

Mary McLeod Bethune

Did You Know

That Mary McLeod Bethune began as a teacher, created the Daytona Normal and Industrial School, now Bethune-Cookman College in Daytona, Florida. It took her 20 years to build the school. Bethune-Cookman College, is a living legacy of Mary McLeod Bethune, it is the only historical Black college founded by a Black woman that continues to thrive today. During the 1930s and 40s, Bethune served as a member of Hoover's National Child Welfare Commission and director of the National Business League, the National Urban League, and president of Roosevelt's Division of Negro Affairs of National Youth Administration. A National memorial was erected in her honor , July 1974, in Washington, D.C.

Black Women Mayors

Match the mayors, present and past in the left hand column with the city they were elected mayor of in the right-hand column.

1.	Mayor Sharon Sayles Belton	a.	Irvington, NJ
2.	Mayor Rosalyn R. Dance	b.	East Point, GA
3.	Mayor Clara K Williams	c.	Petersburg, VA
4.	Mayor Jean L. Harris, M.D.	d.	Evanston, IL
5.	Mayor Sara B. Bost	e.	Minneapolis, MN
6.	Mayor Lorraine H. Morton	f.	Eden Prairie, MN
7.	Mayor Carrie Saxon Perry	g.	Newburgh, NY
8.	Mayor Audrey L. Carey	h.	Riviera Beach, FL
9.	Mayor Sharon Pratt Kelly	i.	Hartford, CT
10.	Mayor Patsy Jo Hilliard	j.	Willingboro, NJ
11.	Mayor Doreatha D. Campbell	k.	Washington, DC
12.	Mayor Charlene Marshall	l.	Taft, OK
13.	Mayor Lelia Smith Foly	m.	Morgantown, WV
14.	Mayor Unita Blackwell	n.	Newport News, VA
15.	Mayor Jessie M. Rattley	o.	Meyersville, MI
16.	Mayor LaMetta K. Wynn	p.	Pasadena, CA
17.	Mayor Loretta T. Glickman	q.	Trinton, NC
18.	Mayor Lottie H. Shackelford	r.	Pageville, MO
19.	Mayor Mary Hall	s.	Little Rock, AR
20.	Mayor Sylvia Willis	t.	Clinton, IA

Answers on page 70/71

Answer Key

Black Mayors

1. Carl Stokes
2. Walter E. Washington
3. Thomas Bradley
4. Coleman Young
5. Atlanta, Georgia
6. Richard Hatcher
7. Andrew Young
8. Harold Washington
9. District of Columbia
10. Wellington E. Webb
11. Charles Evers
12. W. Wilson Goode
13. David Dinkins
14. Birmingham
15. c. Augusta, GA
16. a. Memphis, TN
17. a. Taft, OK
18. a. Newark, NJ
19. James E. Williams, Sr.
20. a. Dwight Tillery
21. c. Howard N. Lee
22. a. Harvey Bernard Gantt
23. a. Theodore Moody Berry
24. a. John McGowan
25. b. Ronald A. Blackwood

Black Firsts

1. a. Cynthia McKinney
2. c. Diane Abbott
3. b. Carlo Moseley-Braum
4. Ronald H. Brown
5. a. Lawrence Douglas Wilder
6. Robert C. Weaver
7. a. Shirley Chisholm
8. Patricia Roberts Harris
9. William Henry Hastie
10. Irving Charles Mollison
11. Charlotta A. Spears
12. a. Edward W. Brooke, III
13. Cardiss Collins
14. William H. Lewis
15. Crystal Byrd Fauset
16. a. Jane M. Bolin
17. c. Edith Sampson
18. a. Medgar Evers
19. b. James Benton Parsons
20. Aris T. Allen
21. b. William L. Clay
22. a. Kweisi Mfume
23. a. Barbara Jordan
24. b. Vernon E. Jordan
25. c. Violette N. Anderson

Who's Who

1. a. Julian Bond
2. Ralph David Abernathy
3. a. Jesse Louis Jackson, Sr.
4. William H. Gray, III
5. Coretta Scott King
6. Marion Shepilov Barry, Jr.
7. b. Roy Ottoway Wilkins
8. Benjamin F. Chavis, Jr.
9. a. Mary Terrell
10. b. Edgar Daniel Nixon

Common Knowledge

1. 1973
2. 1964
3. 1965

Black Women Mayors

1. Sharon Belton - e - Minneapolis, MN
2. Rosalyn Dance - c - Petersburg, VA
3. Clara Williams - h - Riviera Beach, FL

4. Jean Harris - f - Eden Prairie, MN
5. Sara Bost - a - Irvington, NJ
6. Lorraine Morton - d - Evanston, IL
7. Carrie Perry - i - Hartford, CT
8. Audrey Carey - g - Newburgh, NY
9. Sharon P Kelly - k - Washington, DC
10. Patsy Jo Hilliard - b - East Point, GA
11. D. Campbell - j - Willingboro, NJ
12. C. Marshall - m - Morgantown, WV
13. Lelia Foly - l - Taft, OK
14. Unita Blackwell - o - Meyersville, MI
15. J. Rattley - n - Newport News, VA
16. LaMetta Wynn - t - Clinton, IA
17. Loretta Glickman - p - Pasadena, CA
18. L. Shackelford - s - Little Rock, AR
19. Mary Hall - r - Pageville, MO
20. Sylvia Willis - q - Trinton, NC

Sports

BLACK FIRSTS

1. I was named the National Basketball Association (NBA) Most Valuable Player five times, and played in 12 All-Star games. In 1966, while still an active player for the Boston Celtics, I became the first Black American coach in the NBA. As player-coach I led the Celtics to two NBA championships. Who Am I?

   a. Bill Russell c. Wilt Chamberlain
   b. Julius Erving d. Willis Reed

2. In April, 1947, I became the first Black American in Major Leagues since Moses Fleetwood Walker had played in 1885. I was inducted into baseball Hall of Fame in 1962. Who Am I?

   a. Willie Mays c. Jackie Robinson
   b. Bob Gibson d. Ernie Banks

3. I became the first Black American to be named to the American Davis Cup team. In 1968, I became the first Black to win a major tennis title, the National Men's Singles. I was the first Black to win a singles title at Wimbledon in 1975. In 1985, I was inducted into the International Tennis Hall of Fame, becoming the first Black American. I was honored in 1993, by President Bill Clinton, with the Presidential Medal of Freedom. Who Am I?

4. On December 26, 1908, in Sydney, Australia I knocked out Tommy Burns to become the first Black American heavyweight champion. Who Am I?

5. I was the first Black American to play in the Rose Bowl in 1916, for Brown University and in 1919, the first Black to play professional football for a major team, the Akron Indians. Who Am I?

6. I had pitched from 1940, until 1947, for the Chicago American Giants, the Memphis Red Sox, and the Birmingham Black Barons. On August 26, 1947, I became the first Black American pitcher in the National League, to pitch in the major leagues for the Brooklyn Dodgers. Who Am I?

7. On May 26, 1956, I became the first Black American woman to win a major tennis title when I won the women's singles in the French

ANSWERS ON PAGE 100

Open. I won the Wimbledon Championship on July 6, 1957, to become the first Black woman to win. In 1968, I was the first Black woman inducted into the international Tennis Hall of Fame. Who Am I?

a. Althea Gibson
b. Lorraine Williams
c. Zina Garrison
d. Ora Washington

8. On December 18, 1901, I became the first Black American welterweight champion by defeating Rube Ferns, and winning the title in Fort Erie, Ontario. Who Am I?

a. Joe Walcott
b. Thomas Hearns
c. Joe Lashley
d. Jack Johnson

9. I was the first Black American athlete to win the Jim Thorpe Trophy. A football legend at my alma mater Syracuse University, I played football for nine years with the Cleveland Browns and in 1960, I became the first Black to score 126 career touchdowns. I went on to become an actor, sports commentator, and producer. Who Am I?

a. Alan Page
b. Walter Payton
c. Jim Brown
d. Ernie Davis

10. A running back for Syracuse University, in 1961, I became the first Black American Player of The Year, and winner of the Heisman Trophy. I was the first draft pick on both the NFL and the AFL, but I never played professional football after being diagnosed with Leukemia a few days before the college all-star game. Who Am I?

a. Mike Garrett
b. Johnny Rodgers
c. Pat Sullilvan
d. Ernie Davis

11. In 1983, I became the first Black American to sign with the United States Football League, the New Jersey Gremlins. When the USFL collapsed in 1986, I was signed by the Dallas Cowboys. In 1989, I went the Minnesota Vikings. Who Am I?

12. In 1971, I became the first defensive player in the history of the NFL to receive the Most Valuable Player Award. Know as the NFL's Marathon Man, I was the first player to complete a full 26.2 mile marathon. On November 3, 1992, I was elected to the Minnesota Supreme Court. Who Am I?

a. Doug Williams
b. Alan Cedric Page
c. Eric Dickerson
d. Jim Brown

Answers on page 100

Willie Mays & Roy Campanella

Did You Know

That Willie Mays is a member of the Baseball Hall of Fame and ranks third in total career home runs. Known as the "Say Hey Kid," he played in the major leagues for more than 20 years, amassing a record of achievements that rank him among the best ever to have played the game. His 660 home runs give him the third highest all time record, behind only Hank Aaron 755 and Babe Ruth 714. He was inducted into the Baseball Hall of Fame in 1979, the first year in which he was eligible.

13. I became the first Black American to compete against whites in South Africa in the South African PGA Open. In 1974, I became the first Black American to qualify for the Masters tournament and on April 10, 1975, teed off in Atlanta, Georgia as the first Black entry in the Master's. In 1979, I became America's first Black Ryder Cup Team member. Who Am I?
    a. Lee Elder c. Charlie Sifford
    b. Tiger Woods d. Harry Jackson.

14. In 1958, I became the first Black American professional hockey player of the National Hockey League's Boston Bruins. Who Am I?

15. In 1990, I became the first Black woman member of the United States Equestrian Team. I was the first and only equestrienne to be inducted into the Women's Sports Hall of Fame. Who Am I?

16. In 1980, the first Black Americans to participate in the Winter Olympics were Jeff Gadley and Willie Davenport. What was the event they participated in?

17. In the 1948, Olympics held in London, I became the first Black American woman and the only woman to win a gold medal. I took the gold medal in the high jump and set an Olympic record. Who Am I?

18. Formerly of the National Negro League, in 1948, I became the first Black American pitcher in the American League, when I signed with the Cleveland Indians. I also became the first Black to actually pitch in a World Series game. Who Am I?

19. At the National Basketball Association (NBA) annual draft in 1950, I became the first Black American drafted by an NBA team, the Boston Celtics. Who Am I?
    a. Charles Cooper c. Nathaniel Clifton
    b. Wilt Chamberlain d. Earl Lloyd

20. In 1949, I became the National Football League's (NFL) first Black American player from an all Black college, Grambling University. I signed with the Los Angeles Rams, and played for the Rams until 1958. Who Am I?
    a. Kenny Washington c. Paul "Tank" Younger
    b. Willie Thrower d. Jim Brown

ANSWERS ON PAGE 100

21. I am the first Black American to play organized ice hockey. I played for the Atlantic City Seagulls, Eastern Amateur League in 1950. Who Am I?
    a. Willie Thrower
    b. Arthur Dorrington
    c. Atoy Wilson

22. The first Black American college football bowl game was established in 1929. It was played on January 1. What was the name of the bowl?
    a. Prairie View Bowl
    b. Sugar Bowl
    c. Southern Bowl

23. In 1962, I broke a significant color barrier when the Cubs signed me as the first Black American coach on a major league baseball team. I served as chairman of the board of the Negro Leagues Museum in Kansas City, Missouri. Who Am I?
    a. John Jordan O'Neil
    b. Jackie Robinson
    c. Leroy "Satchel" Paige

24. In the 1988, Super Bowl Game XXII, I became the First Black American quarterback to start in a Super Bowl. I played for the Washington Redskins. Who Am I?
    a. Willie Thrower
    b. Doug Williams
    c. Marlin Briscoe

25. I am the first Black American woman figure skater to win a medal in the Winter Olympic Games. I won the bronze medal in the 1988, Games held in Calgary, Canada. Who Am I?
    a. Diane Durham
    b. Andrea Gardiner
    c. Debi Thomas

Answers on page 100

ALTHEA GIBSON

DID YOU KNOW

That Althea Gibson was the first Black American to break the color barrier in professional tennis and the first Black player to win at Wimbledon. After winning at the 1956 French Open, Gibson went on to win five more Grand Slam titles. She also played golf professionally. In 1971, Gibson became the first Black American to be elected to the International Tennis Hall of Fame.

ALSO KNOWN AS

Most athletes seldom escape their career without a nickname. On the following pages, nicknames of star-quality and Hall-of-Fame players are provided and you are ask to identify the real athletes.

	NICKNAME	ATHLETE
1.	*Louisville Lip*	a. William Perry b. Dennis Rodman c. Muhammad Ali
2.	*Mr. Cub*	a. Ernie Banks b. Reggie Jackson c. Willie Mays
3.	*White Shoes*	a. Willie Stargell b. Hank Aaron c. Billy Johnson
4.	*The Human Eraser*	a. Marvin Webster b. George Gervin c. Clyde Drexier
5.	*Bad News*	a. Christian Okoye b. Marvin Barnes c. Darrel Griffith
6.	*Dr. J*	a. Julius Erving b. Karl Malone c. Joe Louis
7.	*The Admiral*	a. Darrel Griffith b. David Robinson c. Clyde Drexler
8.	*Dr. Dunkenstein*	a. Darrel Griffith b. Robert Parish c. Shawn Kemp

ANSWERS ON PAGE 100

9. *The Dream*
   a. Hakeem Olajuwon
   b. Oscar Robertson
   c. Ozzie Smith

10. *The Big O*
    a. Oscar Robertson
    b. Ozzie Smith
    c. Christian Okoye

11. *The Hammer*
    a. Reggie Jackson
    b. Hank Aaron
    c. Ernie Banks

12. *Brown Bomber*
    a. Joe Frazier
    b. Joe Louis
    c. Marvin Hagler

13. *Smokin Joe*
    a. Ed Jones
    b. Joe Frazier
    c. Joe Greene

14. *Magic*
    a. Earwin Johnson
    b. Darryl Dawkins
    c. Wilt Chamberlain

15. *Nigerian Nightmare*
    a. William Perry
    b. David Jones
    c. Christian Okoye

16. *The Iceman*
    a. George Gervin
    b. Clyde Drexler
    c. Earl Monroe

17. *The Fridge*
    a. Joe Greene
    b. Walter Payton
    c. William Perry

18. *Mr. October*
    a. Reggie Jackson
    b. Ernie Banks
    c. Willie Mays

19. *The Glide*
    a. Karl Malone
    b. Antoine Carr
    c. Clyde Drexler

Answers on page 100

20. *The Mailman*
a. David Robinson
b. Julius Erving
c. Karl Malone

21. *Marvelous*
a. Marvin Hagler
b. Joe Frazier
c. Joe Louis

22. *Too Tall*
a. Ed Jones
b. Wilt Chamberlain
c. Bill Russell

23. *The Pearl*
a. Gary Payton
b. Earl Monroe
c. Robert Parish

24. *The Glove*
a. Antoine Carr
b. Gary Payton
c. Ernie Banks

25. *The Worm*
a. Dennis Rodman
b. Shawn Kemp
c. Robert Parish

26. *Big Dog*
a. Marvin Webster
b. Antoine Carr
c. Marvin Barnes

27. *Deacon*
a. David Jones
b. Ed Jones
c. Ernie Banks

28. *Chocolate Thunder*
a. Darryl Dawkins
b. William Perry
c. Joe Frazier

29. *Pops*
a. Willie Stargell
b. Willie Mays
c. Ozzie Smith

30. *Say-Hey-Kid*
a. Willie Mays
b. Reggie Jackson
c. Hank Aaron

Answers on page 100

Kareem Abdul-Jabbar

Kareem Abdul-Jabbar and author Melvett Chambers

Did You Know

That Kareem Abdul - Jabbar (April 16, 1947), was 6 feet 8 inches tall by the time he was 14 years old. While at the University of California Los Angeles (UCLA) he played center and led UCLA to 3 NCAA titles. He was drafted by the Milwaukee Bucks as the first pick, and led the Bucks to a World Championship in his second year, 1971. In 1972, he was traded to the Los Angeles and led the Lakers to five World Championships. After playing for 20 seasons in the NBA, he retired in 1989, as the all time leader in over 20 categories, including playing on 18 All Star teams, and 6 Most Valuable Player awards.

31. *Sweetness*
a. Walter Payton
b. William Perry
c. Ed Jones

32. *Big Dipper*
a. Bill Russell
b. Wilt Chamberlain
c. Shawn Kemp

33. *Human Highlight*
a. Dominique Wilkins
b. Oscar Robertson
c. Gary Payton

34. *Wizard of Oz*
a. Robert Parish
b. Karl Malone
c. Ozzie Smith

35. *Chief*
a. Robert Parish
b. Shawn Kemp
c. Julius Erving

36. *Big E*
a. Earwin Johnson
b. Ewin Hayes
c. Julius Erving

37. *Mean Joe*
a. Joe Greene
b. William Perry
c. Walter Payton

38. *Mr. Basketball*
a. Bill Russell
b. Wilt Chamberlain
c. Ozzie Smith

39. *Reign Man*
a. Robert Parish
b. David Robinson
c. Shawn Kemp

40. *Tiger*
a. Elrick Woods
b. Earl Monroe
c. Clyde Drexler

Answers on page 100

MILESTONES

1. John Roosevelt "Jackie" Robinson (b. January 31, 1919, d. October 24, 1972), four sport athlete at UCLA; baseball, basketball, football and track. On April 15, 1947, Robinson made his debut with the Brooklyn Dodgers at Ebbets Field, to become the first Black American player to compete in modern major league baseball. He was elected to the Baseball Hall of Fame in 1962. His number 42 was retired by every major league club in 1997.

2. Eddie Robinson (b. February 13, 1919). He was head football coach at Grambling College from 1941 to 1997. The winnings coach in college history (408-165-15). He led the Grambling Tigers to 8 national Black college titles.

3. Muhammad Ali (b. Cassius Clay, January 17, 1942). 1960 Olympic light heavyweight champion. He is the only 3-time world heavyweight champ (1964-67, 1974-78, and 1978-79). His career record is 56-5 with 37 KOs and 19 successful title defenses. In 1996, he lit the flaming cauldron to signal the beginning of the Summer Olympics in Atlanta.

4. Florence Griffith Joyner (b. December 21, 1959, d. September 21, 1998). She set world records in track & field 100 and 200 meters in 1988, and won 3 gold medals at the 1988, Olympics, she retired in 1989. In 1993, she was named co-chairperson of the President's Council on Physical Fitness and Sports.

5. Tiger Woods (b December 30, 1975). He became the youngest player at age 18, and the first minority to win the U.S. Amateur in 1994, he won again in 1995, and 1996. He turned pro in September of 1996, and won the fifth event he entered, the Las Vegas Invitational. In his first full year on tour, he won 6 of the 25 events he entered, braking the single season money record. In 1997, he won the Masters by a record 18 under par and 13 stroke margin of victory.

HONORS

1. I was the number one overall pick of the 1968, NBA draft. Known as the "Big E", three-time All-NBA first team 1975, 77, and 79. Twelve-time NBA all star 1969-80, 6th leading scorer in NBA history with 27,313 points, member of NBA Hall of Fame. Who Am I?
   a. Elvin Hayes c. Walt Frazier
   b. Julius Erving d. Elgin Baylor

2. Right hand baseball pitcher, I won 20 or more games 5 times. I won the National League's Cy Young Award 2 times, 1968, and 1970. Most Valuable Player in 1968. I led St. Louis to 2 World Series titles 1964, 67. My win, lost record is 251-174. Who Am I?
   a. Bob Gibson c. Reggie Jackson
   b. Satchel Paige d. Lou Brock

3. I led the NBA in scoring 7 timcs and rebounding 11 times, 7 times All-NBA first team, 4 times Most Valuable Player 1960, 1966-68 in Philadelphia. I scored 100 points against the New York Knicks on March 2, 1962. Who Am I?
   a. Elgin Baylor c. Kareem Abdui-Jabbar
   b. Wilt Chamberlain d. Patrick Ewing

4. I was a 2-time All-American at Kansas. National Football League Rookie of The Year in 1965, and 5-time All-Pro with the Chicago Bears. Who Am I?

NEGRO LEAGUE PLAYERS

- **Andrew "Rube" Foster**
  Career: 1902-1926, Negro League player-manager owner, League executive. No man merits the title of "The father of Black baseball" more then Rube Foster.
- **James "Cool Papa" Bell**
  Career: 1922-1946, Outfield. His speed was legendary "I scored from first base on a single lots of times" Inducted into Hall of Fame in 1979.
- **Josh Gibson**
  Career: 1929-1946, catcher. He was selected to the Cooperstown Hall of Fame in 1972. Titled "The Black Babe Ruth". Played in 11 East-West All Star classics and batted .471.
- **Raymond Dandridge**
  Career: 1933-1949, third base. He was selected to Cooperstown Hall of Fame in 1987.

ANSWERS ON PAGE 100

5. A three time All-American, I led Georgetown to 3 NCAA finals and a 1984 title. NBA Rookie of The Year with New York in 1986, All-NBA in 1990. I was on the U.S. Olympic gold, medal winning teams in 1984 and 1992. I was named one of the NBA's 50 greatest players of all-time. Who Am I?
   a. Julius Erving c. Patrick Ewing
   b. Elvin Hayes d. Michael Jordan

6. I shattered the world record in the 200 meter (19.32 seconds) and set an Olympic record in the 400 meter race, (43.49 seconds) to become the first man to win a gold medal in both races at the same Olympic Games held in Atlanta, GA in 1996. Who Am I?
   a. Michael Johnson c. Bob Hayes
   b. Rafer Johnson d. Carl Lewis

7. I was the world heavyweight champion from June 22, 1937 to March 1, 1949. My reign of 11 years, 8 months is the longest in division history. I successfully defended my title 25 times. I retired in 1949, but returned to the ring in 1950, and lost title shot to Ezzard Charles and then to Rocky Marciano in 1951. My pro record is 63-3 with 49 knockouts. Who Am I?
   a. Sonny Liston c. Sugar Ray Leonard
   b. Joe Louis d. Don King

8. I am the only college football player to win two Heisman Trophies, 1974 and 1975. I rushed for 5,177 yards in my career at Ohio State. Who Am I?
   a. Bo Jackson c. Barry Sanders
   b. Archie Griffin d. Tony Dorsett

NEGRO LEAGUE PLAYERS

- **Lorenzo "Piper" Davis**
  Career: 1942-1952, second base. The first Black American player signed by the Boston Red Sox in 1950. Davis is a former basketball star for the Harlem Globetrotters.
- **Buck O'neil**
  Career: 1937-1955, firstbase. From 1948 to 1955, managed the Kansas City Monarchs to five pennants and two Black World Series.
- **Walter Fenner "Buck" Leonard**
  Career: 1933-1950, voted to the Cooperstown Hall of Fame in 1972.
- **John Henry "Pop" Lloyd**
  Career: 1906-1932, shortstop. After his retirement he served as the little league commissioner in Atlantic City New Jersey. He was inducted into the National Baseball Hall of Fame in 1977.

ANSWERS ON PAGE 100/101

9. I was college player of the year at North Carolina in 1984. I led the National Basketball Association (NBA) in scoring 7 years in a row, 1987-95, and 1996-98. 5 time regular season MVP; 1988, 1991-92, 1998, and 6 times Most Valuable Player in NBA finals; 1991-93, 1996-98. 3 time AP Male Athlete of The Year. Led the U.S. Olympic team to gold medals in 1984 and 92. I led the Chicago Bulls to 6 NBA titles. Who Am I?
   a. Michael Jordan
   b. Julius Erving
   c. Scottie Pippen
   d. Elgin Baylor

10. I won the Heisman Trophy in 1985 and the Most Valuable Player of the baseball All-Star Game in 1989. I started for both baseball's KC Royals and NFL's LA Raiders in 1988 and 1989. Who Am I?

11. This Black American rodeo cowboy is generally credited with being the first person to develop a way of bulldogging that made the act a spectacular performance. On December 9, 1971, he became the first Black American to be elected to the National Rodeo Cowboy Hall of Fame. What is his name?
   a. Nat Love
   b. Charles Sampson
   c. Bill Pickett
   d. Jim Davis

12. I won the Heisman Trophy as a junior at Oklahoma State in 1988. All time NCAA single season leader in rushing, 2,628 yards. Four time National Football League's (NFL) rushing leader with Detroit Lions, 1990, 1994, 1996 and 1997. NFC Rookie of The Year in 1988. Two time NFL Player of The Year 1991, 97. Who Am I?
   a. Deion Sanders
   b. Tony Dorsett
   c. Bo Jackson
   d. Barry Sanders

NEGRO LEAGUE PLAYERS

- **Martin Dihigo**
  Career: 1923-1945, outfield. He was selected to the Cooperstown Hall of Fame in 1977. The only player elected to baseball Halls of Fame in three countries: The United States, Cuba and Mexico.

- **Willie Foster**
  Career: 1923-1938, pitcher. Left hand pitcher with a great fastball and devastating change up, he was the best pitcher in the original Negro National League. After his retirement, he served as baseball coach and dean of men at Alcorn State University in, Mississippi. Foster was inducted into the Hall of Fame in 1996.

ANSWERS ON PAGE 101

13. At the 1960, Olympics, I won three gold medals; 100 meter, 200 meter and 4x100 meter relay. I also won a silver medal in the 1956, Games. I was AP Athlete of The Year 2 times; 1960, and 61, and winner of the Sullivan Award in 1961. Who Am I?
 a. Wyomia Tyus c. Wilma Glodean Rudolph
 b. Willye Brown White d. Valerie Brisco-Hooks

14. This Black American won a silver medal in the 1956, Olympic decathlon and a gold medal in the decathlon at the 1960, Olympics. What is his name?

15. Black American baseball player, three time National League Most Valuable Player; 1951, 1953 and 1955, I led the Brooklyn Dodgers to 5 pennants and the 1st World Series title in 1955. My career was cut short when a car accident in 1958, left me paralyzed in both my arms and legs. I was inducted to the Hall of Fame in 1969. Who Am I?

16. On July 8, 1924, I became the first Black American in Olympic history to win an individual gold medal. I won the broad jump with a leap of 25 feet 5 1/2 inches. Who Am I?

17. I was the first Black American from a Black college to win an Olympic medal. I won a gold medal at the 1956 Olympics held in Melbourne and again in 1960 at the Rome Olympics, both in the 110 meter hurdles. I became the first athlete to win this event twice. Who Am I?
 a. Edwin Moses c. Rafer Johnson
 b. Cornelius Johnson d. Lee Quincy Calhoun

NEGRO LEAGUE PLAYERS

• Oscar Charleston
Career: 1915-1954, center field, first base, manager. In 1921, he batted .434 in 60 league games while leading the Negro National League in doubles, triples, home runs and stolen bases. His career spanned virtually the entire history of the Negro Leagues. In 1976, he was inducted into the Baseball Hall of Fame.

• Satchel Paige
Career: 1926-1950, pitcher. A great story teller and one of the greatest pitcher in baseball history. Paige closed out his career in 1965 by pitching 3 scoreless innings for the Kansas City Athletics at age 59, becoming the oldest man to pitch in a major league game. He was inducted into the Hall of Fame in 1971.

ANSWERS ON PAGE 101

18. In the 1904 Olympic Games held in St. Louis, Missouri, I finished third in the 400 meter hurdles and fourth in the 400 meter dash, becoming the first Black American to win a medal in the Olympic Games. Who Am I?

19. On May 25, 1935, I made history at Ohio State University. I broke five world records in one afternoon at a Big Ten Championship track and field meet. A year later, I won four gold medals at the 1936, Olympic Games held in Berlin, where I upstaged Hitler, who had hoped to prove that the Germans were the master race. At the opening ceremony of the 1984 Olympics in Los Angeles, my granddaughter, Hemphill, carried the Olympic torch into the coliseum as a tribute to my memory. Who Am I?
    a. Archie Williams
    b. John Woodruff
    c. Jesse Owens
    d. Cornelius Johnson

20. In 1984, I won four Olympic gold medals; (100 meter, 200 meter, 4x100 meter and the long jump), two in 1988, (100 meter and the long jump), two in 1992, (4x100 meter and long jump) and one in 1996, (long jump). I have a record eight World Championship titles and nine medals in all. I was the winner of the Sullivan Award in 1981, and two-time AP Male Athlete of the Year; 1983 and 1984. Who Am I?
    a. Rafer Johnson
    b. Edwin Moses
    c. Carl Lewis
    d. Jesse Owens

Negro League Players

• **Willie Wells**
Career: 1924-1949, shortstop, although his arm was not strong, Wells was the first shortstop in baseball history to combine dazzling fielding with home run power. In 1926, he hit 27 home runs in 88 games for the St. Louis Stars. The Negro National League single season record. He was elected to the Hall of Fame in 1997.

• **Wilbur "Bullet" Rogan**
Career: 1917-1938, pitcher, outfield, manager. He begin his Negro League career in 1920, at age 30 when he join the Kansas City Monarchs, after serving nine years in the U.S. Army. He was recommended to the Monarchs by Casey Stengel, so the story goes. Rogan's best season in the Negro League was in 1924, at age 35.

Answers on page 101

NEGRO LEAGUE TEAMS

From 1872 to the 1950s there were over 100 semi-professional and professional all Black baseball teams made up of over 4000 players. The teams below are by no means a complete list of all the teams that made up the Negro baseball league.

Atlanta Black Crackers
Negro National League 1938

Baltimore Black Sox
Eastern Colored League 1923

Birmingham Black Barons
Negro National League 1924

Brooklyn Royal Giants
Eastern Colored League 1923

Chatenooga Black Lookouts
Negro Southern League

Chicago American Giants
Negro National League 1920

Cleveland Buckeyes
Negro American League 1943

Dayton Marcos
Negro National League 1920

Detroit Stars
Negro National League 1920

Detroit Wolves
Negro East West League

Houston Eagles
Negro American League 1949

Indianapolis ABC's
Negro National League 1920

Indianapolis Clowns
Negro American League 1944

Jacksonville Red Caps
Negro American League 1938

Kansas City Monarchs
Negro National League 1920

Memphis Red Sox
Negro National League 1924

Montgomery Grey Sox
Negro Southern League 1932

Newark Eagles
Negro National League 1936

New York Black Yankees
Negro National League 1936

New York Cubans
Negro National League 1935

Nashville Elite Giants
Negro National League 1930

Philadelphia Stars
Negro National Legaue 1934

Pittsburgh Crawfords
Negro National League 1933

Saint Louis Stars
Negro National League 1920

Seattle Steelheads
West Coast Negro Baseball League

Washington Potomacs
Eastern Colored League

Common Knowledge

The following events and performances all occurred in the same year. Can you identify the year?

1.
- Arthur Ashe wins the U.S. Open tennis championships at Forest Hills, New York.
- Bob Foster knocks out Dick Tiger in four rounds to win the light heavyweight championship.
- O.J. Simpson is named the Heisman Trophy winner.
- Marlin Briscoe of the Denver Broncos is the first Black American quarterback to play regularly in professional football.

The year was: 1967 1968 1970

2.
- Nell Jackson is the first Black American to sit on the U.S. Olympic Committee's board of directors. She is later inducted into the Black Athletes Hall of Fame.
- Tina Sloane-Green is the first Black American woman to compete on the U.S. National Lacrosse team.
- John B. Mclendon becomes the first Black American coach in the American Basketball League when he signs a two-year contract with the Cleveland Pipers.
- Uriah Jones is the first Black American member on a U.S. Olympic fencing team.

The year was: 1958 1969 1975

3.
- Gale Sayers, running back for the Chicago Bears is elected to the National Football Hall of Fame.
- Reggie Jackson of the New York Yankees is the first baseball player to hit three home runs in a World Series game.
- Earl Campbell, University of Texas, fullback is named the Heisman Trophy winner.
- Ernie Banks is elected to the National Baseball Hall of Fame.

The year was: 1972 1975 1977

Answers on page 101

Black Coaches

Match the coaches in the left hand column with the team they are/or have been head coach of in the right hand column.

1.	Tony Dungy	a. Arkansas
2.	Dennis Green	b. Georgetown
3.	Ray Rhodes	c. Temple
4.	Bob Simmons	d. Hampton University
5.	Willie Jeffries	e. Southern University
6.	William Hayes	f. Grambling State
7.	Joe Taylor	g. Boston Celtics
8.	Pete Richardson	h. Minnesota Vikings
9.	Doug Williams	i. Tampa Bay
10.	Eddie Robinson	j. Green Bay Packers
11.	Art Shell	k. Oklahoma State
12.	Nolan Richardson	l. South Carolina State
13.	John Chaney	m. North Carolina A & T
14.	John Thompson	n. Los Angeles Raiders
15.	Bill Russell	o. Grambling State
16.	Herman Edwards	p. San Jose State
17.	Tyrone Willingham	q. Seattle Super Sonics
18.	Fitz Hall	r. Orlando Magic
19.	Maurice Cheeks	s. Charlotte Hornets
20.	Isiah Thomas	t. New Jersey Nets
21.	Paul Silas	u. New York Jets
22.	Sylvester Croom	v. Indiana Pacers
23.	Fritz Pollard	w. Notre Dame
24.	Byron Scott	x. Mississippi State
25.	Doc Rivers	y. Akron

Answers on page 101

Jesse Owens

Did You Know

That Jesse Owens (September 12, 1913 - March 31, 1980), Black American sprinter was the winner of 4 gold medals in the 1936, Olympic Games. In his time he was heralded as "The world's fastest human." In college at Ohio State, Owens won 42 events, including four in the Big Ten Championships, four in NCAA Championships and three at the Olympic trials. At the 1936, Olympics Owens won an unprecedented four gold medals; the 100 meters, 200 meters, 400 meter relay and the long jump, he set a record that would last for 25 years. Owens received no official recognition for his feat in the United States until 40 years after the fact, when he was awarded a 1976, Presidential Medal of Freedom.

MEMORABLE MOMENTS

1. Name the only two coaches who played on a NCAA championship team and coached a NBA championship team. They were also teammates, both played in the NBA
   a. Lenny Wilkens and Bernie Bickerstaff
   b. Bill Russell and K.C. Jones
   c. Earvin "Magic" Johnson and K.C. Jones

2. Name the only man to play for a NBA championship team and coach a NCAA Tournament champion.
   a. Nolan Richardson
   b. John Chaney
   c. John Thompson

3. I was head football coach at Division I-AA from 1941 to 1997. The winningest coach in college history, 408-165-15, led the Tigers to 8 national Black colleges titles. Who Am I?
   a. Eddie Robinson
   b. Alonzo Smith
   c. Willie Jefferies

4. I was the first Black American to win boxing titles in five weight classes. Who Am I?
   a. Thomas "Hit Man" Hearns
   b. Sugar Ray Robinson
   c. Emile Griffith

5. In 1980, Maury Willis was named manager of what major league baseball team?
   a. Seattle Mariners
   b. Chicago Cubs
   c. Brooklyn Dodgers

6. In 1972, I became the first player in the NBA to score 30,000 points when I played in a game between the Los Angeles Lakers and the Phoenix Suns. Who Am I?
   a. Magic Johnson
   b. Bill Russell
   c. Wilt Chamberlain

ANSWERS ON PAGE 101

7. On November 30, 1956, I knocked out Archie Moore in the fifth round to become the youngest heavyweight champion at age 21. Who Am I?
   a. Floyd Patterson
   b. Joe Frazier
   c. Joe Louis

8. In 1957, this university won it first NAIA title, becoming the first Black college to win a national title. Name the university.
   a. Tennessee State University
   b. Grambling University
   c. Prairie View A & M

9. On May 1, 1991 Ricky Henderson of the Oakland A's broke Lou Brock's all-time record of bases stole to become the all-time leader. How many bases did he steal?
   a. 939
   b. 927
   c. 896

10. In the 1988, Summer Olympics held in Los Angeles, Calif. I won three gold medals and one silver medal, becoming the first American woman to win four medals. Who Am I?
   a. Florence Griffith-Joyner
   b. Valerie Brisco-Hooks
   c. Jacqueline Joyner-Kersee

11. On February 10, 1990, in Tokyo Japan, James "Buster" Douglas knocked out this heavyweight champion in a major upset to become the heavyweight champion. Who did he KO?
   a. Michael Spinks
   b. Mike Tyson
   c. James Smith

12. In 1947, the Cleveland Indians of the American League bought my baseball contract from the Newark Eagles of the Negro National League. I played my first game for the Indians on July 4, 1947, eleven weeks after Jackie Robinson broke the color barrier by playing for the Brooklyn Dodgers in the National League. Though I was the second Black American in the Major Leagues, I was the first in the American League. In March 1998, I was inducted into baseball's Hall of Fame. Who Am I?

ANSWERS ON PAGE 101

Bill Pickett

Did You Know

That Bill Pickett (December 5, 1870?-April 2, 1932), cowboy and rodeo star invented and popularized "bulldogging", a method of steer-wrestling to bring a bull to the ground. In 1971, the National Rodeo Cowboy Hall of Fame inducted Pickett as its first Black American honoree, and in 1994, he appeared on a commemorative postage stamp.

13. In 1981, boxer Sugar Ray Leonard is named Sportsman of The Year by this magazine.
    a. Sports Illustrated
    b. Ebony
    c. Jet

14. September 15, 1978, Muhammad Ali regains the WBA heavyweight title after defeating this boxer in New Orleans, LA. Ali becomes the first heavyweight boxer to win the championship title three times. Who was the boxer?
    a. Larry Holmes
    b. Joe Frazier
    c. Leon Spinks

15. The first known Black American to play professional football signed with the Shelby Athletic Club of Shelby, Ohio in 1902. He was a running back. What is his name?

16. Name this professional basketball player, popularly known as "Dr. J", innovator of the slam-dunk, and one of the most electrifying players to play the game. In 1993, he was inducted into the Basketball Hall of Fame.
    a. Michael Jordan
    b. Julius Erving
    c. Magic Johnson

17. She is one of the greatest female basketball players to play the game. A four-time All-American in high school, she scored 105 points in a single high school game in 1982. Her high school had a win-loss record of 132-4 during her four years there. She finished her collegiate career with an average of 23.6 points and 12 rebounds per game, and during her four years at USC, the team had a win-loss record of 112-20. She was the first basketball player at USC, male or female to have a jersey number retired. In 1995, she was inducted into the Basketball Hall of Fame. What is her name?

18. A Dallas Cowboy star, in 1995, I rushed for a record 25 touchdowns to broke the 12 year old record of Hall of Famer, John Riggins. Who Am I?

19. In 1973, while playing for Buffalo, I became the first 2,000 yard single season rusher in NFL history. Who Am I?

Answers on page 101

20. Name the only pro player to appear in both a World Series and a Super Bowl.
    a. Bo Jackson
    b. Dejon Sanders
    c. Barry Sanders

21. I was called the "World's Fastest Human", a two time gold medallist at the 1964 Tokyo Summer Olympics, and played wide receiver for the Dallas Cowboys. Who Am I?
    a. Bob Hayes
    b. Carl Lewis
    c. Jim Brown

22. The Twin Towers anchored the Houston Rocket's front court from 1984-85 through 1987-88. What is their names?
    a. Ralph Sampson, Hakeem Olajuwon
    b. Bill Russell, Wilt Chamberlain
    c. Karl Malone, Gary Payton

23. The Three Amigos were speedy wide receivers who played for the Denver Broncos on the 1987, and 1989 Super Bowl teams. What is their names?

24. I helped lead the Raiders to 2 Super Bowl titles in 1976 and 1980. I am executive director of the National Football League Players Association. I was elected to the Pro Football Hall of Fame in 1971. Who Am I?
    a. Bo Jackson
    b. Art Shell
    c. Gene Upshaw

25. In 1967, I became the first Black American to be elected to Pro Football Hall of Fame. I played defensive back for the New York Giants 1949-1958 and Green Bay Packers 1959-1961. Who Am I?
    a. Emlen Tunnell
    b. Lawrence Taylor
    c. Walter Playton

ANSWERS ON PAGE 101

Answer Key

Black First

1. Bill Russell
2. Jackie Robinson
3. Arthur Ashe
4. Jack Johnson
5. Friz Pollard
6. Dan Bankhead
7. Althea Gibson
8. Joe Walcott
9. Jim Brown
10. Ernie Davis
11. Herschel Walker
12. Alan Cedric Page
13. Lee Elder
14. Willie O'Rhee
15. Donna Cheek
16. Bobsled Team
17. Alice Coachman
18. Leroy "Satchel" Paige
19. Charles Cooper
20. Paul "Tank" Younger
21. b. Arthur Dorrington
22. a. The Prairie View Bowl
23. a. John "Buck" Jordan O'Neil
24. b. Doug Williams
25. c. Debi Thomas

Also Known As

1. c. Muhammad Ali
2. a. Ernie Banks
3. c. Billy Johnson
4. a. Marvin Webster
5. b. Marvin Barnes
6. a. Julius Erving
7. b. David Robinson
8. a. Darrel Griffith
9. a. Hakeem Olajuwon
10. a. Oscar Robertson
11. b. Hank Aaron
12. b. Joe Louis
13. b. Joe Frazier
14. a. Earwin Johnson
15. c. Christian Okoye
16. a. George Gervin
17. c. William Perry
18. a. Reggie Jackson
19. c. Clyde Drexler
20. c. Karl Malone
21. a. Marvin Hagler
22. a. Ed Jones
23. b. Earl Monroe
24. b. Gary Payton
25. a. Dennis Rodman
26. b. Antoine Carr
27. a. David Jones
28. a. Darryl Dawkins
29. a. Willie Stargell
30. a. Willie Mays
31. a. Walter Payton
32. b. Wilt Chamberlain
33. a. Dominique Wilkins
34. c. Ozzie Smith
35. a. Robert Parish
36. b. Elvin Hayes
37. a. Joe Greene
38. a. Bill Russell
39. c. Shawn Kemp
40. a. Elrick Woods

Honors

1. a. Elvin Hayes
2. a. Bob Gibson
3. b. Wilt Chamberlain
4. Gale Sayers
5. c. Patrick Ewing
6. a. Michael Johnson
7. b. Joe Louis

8. b. Archie Griffin
9. a. Michael Jordan
10. Bo Jackson
11. c. Bill Pickett
12. d. Barry Sanders
13. c. Wilma Glodean Rudolph
14. Rafer Johnson
15. Roy Campanella
16. William DeHart Hubbard
17. d. Lee Quincy Calhoun
18. George Poage
19. c. Jesse Owens
20. c. Carl Lewis

Common Knowledge

1. 1968
2. 1969
3. 1977

Black Coaches

1. Tony Dungy -i- Tampa Bay
2. Dennis Green -h- Minnesota Vikings
3. Ray Rhodes -j- Green Bay Packers
4. Bob Simmons -k- Oklahoma State
5. Willie Jeffries-l-South Carolina State
6. William Hayes-m-North Carolina A&T
7. Joe Taylor -d- Hampton University
8. Pete Richardson-e-Southern University
9. Doug Williams -f- Grambling State
10. Eddie Robinson -o- Grambling State
11. Art Shell -n- LA Raiders
12. Nolan Richardson -a- Arkansas
13. John Chaney -c- Temple
14. John Thompson -b- Georgetown
15. Bill Russell -g- Boston Celtics
16. Herman Edwards -u- New York Jets
17. Tyrone Willingham -w- Notre Dame
18. Fitz Hall -p- San Jose State
19. Maurice Cheeks-q-Seattle Super Sonics
20. Isiah Thomas -v- Indiana Pacers
21. Paul Silas -s- Charlotte Hornets
22. Sylvester Croom -x- Mississippi State
23. Fritz Pollard -y- Akron
24. Byron Scott -t- New Jersey Nets
25. Doc Rivers -r- Orlando Magic

Memorable Moments

1. b. Bill Russell and K.C. Jones
2. c. John Thompson
3. a. Eddie Robinson
4. a. Thomas "Hit Man" Hearns
5. a. Seattle Mariners
6. c. Wilt Chamberlain
7. a. Floyd Patterson
8. a. Tennessee State University
9. a. 939
10. a. Florence Griffith-Joyner
11. b. Mike Tyson
12. Lawrence Day
13. a. Sports Illustrated
14. c. Leon Spinks
15. Charles W. Follis
16. b. Julius Erving
17. Cheryl Miller
18. Emmitt Smith
19. O. J. Simpson
20. b. Dejon Sanders
21. a. Bob Hayes
22. a. Ralph Sampson, Hakeem Olajuwon
23. Vance Johnson, Ricky Nattiel, and Mark Jackson
24. c. Gene Upshaw
25. a. Emlen Tunnell

Inventions Science & Medicine

BLACK INVENTORS

Passage of the Thirteenth and fourteenth Amendments to the Constitution brought unrecognized benefits to Black Americans, one of those benefits gave Black American the right to patent her or her inventions. As a result of this, the period following the Civil War saw the number of patents for inventions filed by Blacks increase dramatically. However, we do not know exactly how many patents were obtained by Black Americans since racial identity was not recorded by the patent office.

One can only speculate on the significant part Black Americans played in inventions they are known to have worked on. Between 1870, and 1900, though some 80% of Black adults in the United States were illiterate, Blacks were awarded several hundred patents.

1. In 1901, I patented my first invention, an improvement on the sewing machine, which I then sold for $150. On July 25, 1916, me and three others demonstrated the effectiveness of my "gas inhalator" by saving more than twenty men who were trapped by a tunnel explosion. Seven years later, my traffic light received a U.S. patent on November 20, 1923 and was patented in Great Britain and Canada. My design was so successful that General Electric paid me $40,000 for the rights to my automatic traffic signal. Who Am I?
   a. Garrett A. Morgan
   b. Shelby J. Davidson
   c. Granville T. Woods

2. I invented the air conditioning unit, patented July 12, 1949. Who Am I?
   a. Elijah McCoy
   b. Frederick M. Jones
   c. Jan Matzeliger

3. The automatic gear shift, patented December 6, 1932 patent number 1,889,814 was invented by who?
   a. Richard B. Spikes
   b. Frederick M. Jones
   c. Garrett A. Morgan

ANSWERS ON PAGE 116

4. Some of my inventions and patents included the automatic water feeder, 1920; automobile indicator, 1921; thermostat setting apparatus, 1928; vacuum heating system, 1929; and the vacuum pump, 1939. I had at least 34 U.S. patents and 80 foreign ones relating to the design, installation, testing and servicing of power plants, heating and ventilating systems. Who Am I?
   a. Frederick M. Jones
   b. David N. Crosthwait, Jr.
   c. Andrew J. Beard

5. I invented the thermostatic control hair curlers, patented August 8, 1953, patent number 2,648,757. Who Am I?
   a. Solomon Harper
   b. Henry Blair
   c. Granville T. Woods

6. I was responsible for more than a hundred patents. The following are just a few; electric railway system, July 9, 1901; regulating and controlling electrical translating devices, September 3, 1901; automatic air brake, June 10, 1902; electric railway, May 26, 1903. Who Am I?
   a. Richard B. Spikes
   b. Granville T. Woods
   c. Garrett A. Morgan

7. As chief chemist and director of research for Griffith Laboratories of Chicago, I discovered curing salts for the preserving and processing of meats, thus revolutionizing the meat-packing industry. I have more than 100 patents registered for processes used in the manufacturing and packing of food products. Who Am I?
   a. Henry A. Hill
   b. Frederick M. Jones
   c. Lloyd A. Hall

8. I invented an airplane safety device, patent May 24, 1921, patent number 1,379,264. Who Am I?
   a. Hubert Julian
   b. Richard B. Spikes
   c. Henry Blair

Answers on page 116

9. The term "the Real McCoy" comes from the automatic engine lubricator of this inventor, designed to continuously oil train and ship engines, which was immediately adopted by railroad and shipping lines. In April 1915, I received a patent for a graphite lubricator that eliminated the problems of oiling the super heater engine that used large amounts of steam to operate. In 1920, I established the Elijah McCoy Manufacturing Company to manufacture and sell the lubricator. Who Am I?

10. I patent the first cost efficient method for producing carbon filaments for electric lights. I made patent drawings for many of Alexander Graham Bell's telephone patents and worked for the United States Electric Lighting Company. On August 10, 1910, I patent the lamp fixture. Who Am I?
    a. Lewis H. Latimer
    b. Jan Matzeliger
    c. Granville T. Woods

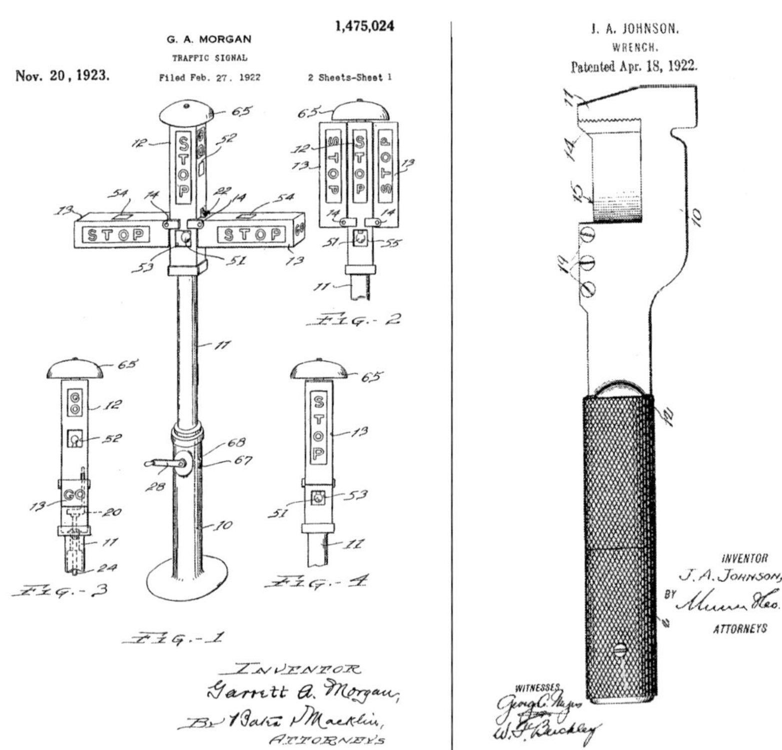

ANSWERS ON PAGE 116

11. I invented the check row corn planter, patented January 16, 1900, patent number 641,462. Who Am I?
    a. Otis Boykin
    b. Lewis Temple
    c. J.M. Mitchell

12. The man powered glider aircraft, patented February 6, 1973, patent number 3,715,011 was invented by me. Who Am I?
    a. G.B. Prather
    b. Grainville T. Wood
    c. Frederick M. Jones

13. I am one of two naval research laboratory persons responsible for the Apollo 16 lunar surface ultraviolet camera spectrograph, which was placed on the lunar surface in April, 1972. It was I who designed the instrument. I received my Ph.D. in physics from the University of Illinois in 1964. I am the recipient of the National Aeronautical Space Agency's Exceptional Scientific Achievement Medal for my work on the ultraviolet camera/spectrograph. Who Am I?
    a. George E. Carruthers
    b. Lewis Temple
    c. Richard B. Spikes

14. On January 21, 1919, I received a patent number, 1,292,330 for "The Jones" vehicle spring, a mechanism to raise and lower a top for an automobile. Who Am I?
    a. James A. Jones
    b. Grainville T. Woods
    c. Frederick M. Jones

15. This inventor was responsible for the following inventions; the modern version of the railroad semaphore, 1906; the automatic car washer and auto directional signals, 1913; the beer keg tap, 1910; the continuous contact trolley pole for electric railways, 1919; combination milk bottle opener and bottle cover, June 29, 1926, patent number 1,590,557; automatic shoe shine chair, around 1939; multiple barrel machine gun, 1940. What is his name?
    a. Garrett A. Morgan
    a. Joseph H. Smith
    b. Richard. Spikes

ANSWERS ON PAGE 116

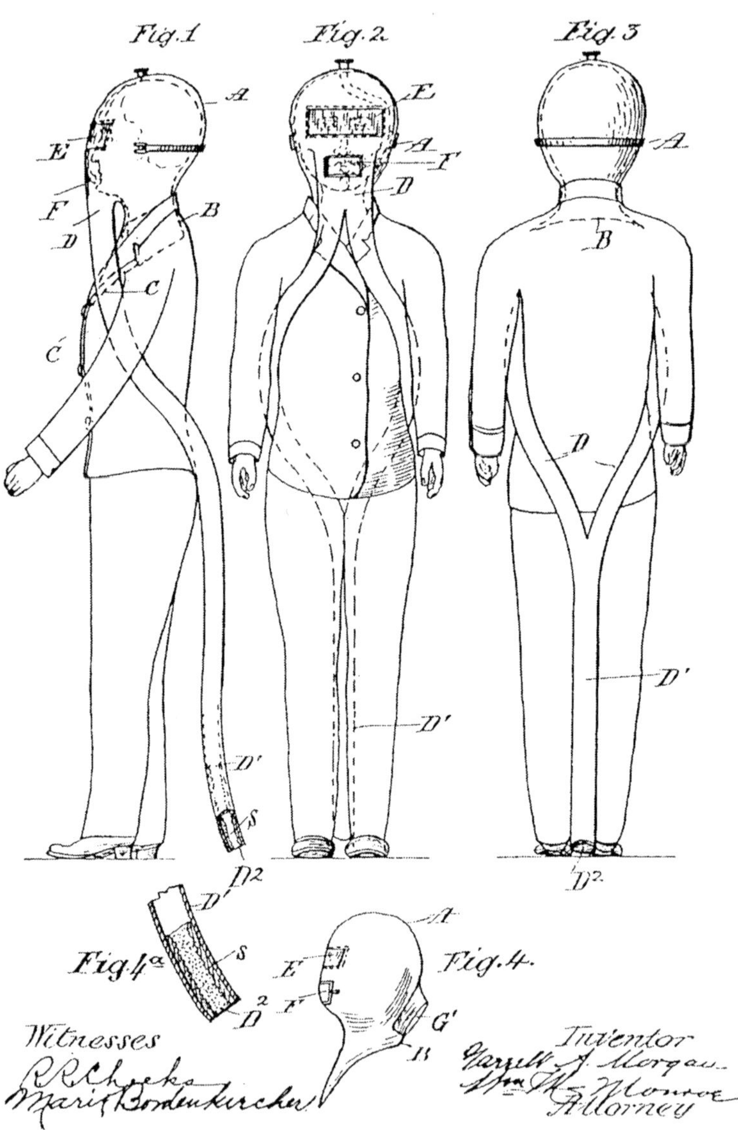
G. A. MORGAN.
BREATHING DEVICE.
APPLICATION FILED AUG. 19, 1912.
1,113,675.
Patented Oct. 13, 1914.
2 SHEETS—SHEET 1.
Fig. 1
Fig. 2
Fig. 3
Fig. 4a
Fig. 4.
Witnesses
Inventor
Attorney

COMMON KNOWLEDGE

The following achievements and contributions all occurred in the same year. Can you identify the year?

1.
- Davis N. Crosthwait, Jr. invented and patent an automatic water feeder, he later invent an automobile indicator, a thermostat-setting apparatus, and a vacuum heating system.
- The Universal African Black Cross nurses was organized as a female auxiliary of the Universal Negro Improvement Association

The year was: 1920 1928 1932

2.
- Louis Wright became the first Black American physician to be appointed to a predominantly white hospital staff, he was appointed clinical assistant visiting surgeon at Harlem Hospital, in New York City.
- Fannie Elliott officially became the first Black nurse to be recognized by the American Red Cross.
- Alice Parker received a patent for a heating furnace that uses gas instead of coal for fuel.
- Dr. William A. Hinton was appointed lecturer in preventive medicine & hygiene at Harvard Medical School.

The year was: 1919 1932 1948

3.
- Percy Julian presented two papers before the American Chemical Society, his work on the precursors of a drug known as physostigmine attracted the attention of both American and European scientists.
- Louis Wright became the second Black American member of the American College of Surgeons.
- Leonidas H. Berry became the first Black American specialist in the field of digestive diseases and endosopy. He wrote *"I Wouldn't Take Nothin' for My Journey."*

The year was: 1920 1934 1948

ANSWERS ON PAGE 116

BLACK FIRSTS

1. On March 31, 1963, I became the first Black American astronaut candidate. Who Am I?

2. In September, 1993, I was confirmed by the U.S. Senate, and became the first Black American to serve as surgeon general of the United states. Who Am I?

3. In 1977, I became the first Black American president of the American Chemical Society and chaired the chemistry section of the American Association for the Advancement of Science. Who Am I?

4. I am one of only 30 women to enter the Massachusetts Institute of Technology (MIT) in 1964. I earned a B.S. degree in 1968 and a Ph. D. in 1973, from MIT, making me the first Black American to earn a doctorate from MIT. In 1991, I became a professor in the Department of Physics at Rutgers University. In 1995, I became the first Black American chairperson of the U.S. Nuclear Regulatory Commission. Who Am I?

5. In 1945, I became the first Black American nurse to be commissioned in the Navy Reserve Corps. Who Am I?

6. In 1980, this Black American doctor performs the first surgical implantation of the automatic implant able defibrillator in the human heart. What is his name?

7. Physician and chemical engineer, I am the first Black American woman astronaut. I got my M.D. from Cornell Medical School. In 1992, I became the first Black women in space. Who Am I?

8. In 1922, I was named medical officer-chief of the Veterans Hospital in Tuskegee, Alabama. I became the first Black American appointed to head a Veterans Administration hospital. Who Am I?

9. In 1916, I became the first Black American to receive a Ph.D. in chemistry from the University of Illinois. Who Am I?

ANSWERS ON PAGE 116

George Washington Carver

Did You Know

That George Washington Carver was a Black American agriculturist, educator and inventor know for the development of peanut products. He graduated from Iowa State in 1884 with a degree in botany and agriculture, earned his master's, then became head of the department of Scientific Agriculture at Tuskegee Institute in 1896. He developed over 300 peanut products. In 1921, he helped the United Peanut Growers Association persuade Congress to pass a bill calling for a protective tariff on imported peanuts. Carver only patented three of his 500 agriculture inventions, saying "God gave them to me, how can I sell them to someone else?" He died January 4, 1943, in Tuskegee, Ala.

10. In 1949, William Augustus became the first Black American professor at this medical school. What was the school?

11. Name the first Black American to be appointed to the Atomic Energy Commission.

12. In 1983, I became the first Black American astronaut to orbit the earth. Who Am I?

13. I was the first Black American physician to be appointed to the staff of a New York municipal hospital, the first Black American surgeon to be admitted to the American College of Surgeons, and the first Black American physician in America to head a public interracial hospital. Who Am I?

14. I am the first Black American to obtain a doctorate in astronomy. I earn my Ph.D. from Georgetown University in 1961. Who Am I?

15. In 1993, I became the first Black American director of the Centers for Disease Control. Who Am I?

16. I received my bachelor of science degree in 1930, from the University of Illinois and my medical degree from the University of Illinois's College if Medicine in 1934. I became the first Black American to be admitted as a fellow of the American College of Surgeons. Who Am I?

17. In 1902, I became the first Black American woman licensed to practice medicine in the Denver, Colorado area. I delivered over 7,000 babies and became known as the "Baby Doctor." Who Am I?

18. I graduate from Florida A&M in 1941 and Howard University School of Medicine in 1944, and in 1949, I became the first Black American cancer surgeon at Sloan Kettering Hospital. Who Am I?

19. I was the first Black American to be elected to the National Academy of Sciences. I pioneered the study of mathematical game theory and in 1979, I received the Von Neumann Theory prize. Who Am I?

20. In 1990, I became the first Black American woman to serve as president of the American Medical Association. Who Am I?

Answers on page 116

Did You Know

1. That Walter E. Massey, earned a Ph.D. in physics from Washington University in 1966. After serving as a professor of physics at Brown University from 1973 to 1979, he was appointed director of the Argonne Laboratory, where he manages a staff of 5,000 and an annual budget of nearly $250 million. In 1991, he became the first Black American to be named director of the National Science Foundation.

2. That James A. Harris earned a B.S. in chemistry in 1953, was a member of the team that identified two new elements; Unnilquadium (104) and Unnilpentium (105), in 1969 and 1970. In 1977, Harris became head of Lawrence Berkeley's Engineering and Technical Services Division.

3. That Ernest J. Wilkins, Jr. received a Ph.D. in physics from the University of Chicago at age 19. Then studied mechanical engineering at New York University, taught mathematics at Tuskegee University, and took part in the research that led to the development of the atomic bomb. He is known for developing techniques for measuring the absorption of gamma radiation emitted for the sun.

4. That Emmett W. Chappelle, conducted research at Stanford University from 1958 to 1963. Worked as Hazelton Laboratories as a biochemist, exobiologist, and astrochemist. In 1977, he took a position at NASA's Goddard Space Flight Center. Chappelle along with Grace Piccolo developed a method for the immediate detection of bacteria in water.

5. That Clive O. Callender earned degrees in chemistry and psychology from Hunter College, in New York in 1959. He entered Meharry College in Nashville, Tennessee and graduated first in his class in 1963. He became the first Black American transplant surgeon at the University of Minnesota Hospital. Callender joined the faculty of the Howard University Medical school in 1973.

WHO'S WHO

1. I studied engineering physics at Cornell were I received a B.S. in 1953 and the California Institute of Technology where I received my Ph.D. in 1960. My work produced new techniques for removing smoke from buildings and dispersing fog on airport runways. I invented the focus-flow heat sink, which is used for cooling computer chips. I established my own laboratory in 1964, employing 150 staff members. In 1994, I was inducted into the Engineering and Science Hall of Fame. Who Am I?
   a. Meredith Gourdine
   b. Walter E. Massey
   c. Lewis Howard Latimer

2. I graduated Magna Cum Laude from Dartmouth College in 1907 and earned a Ph.D. in zoology from University of Chicago in 1916. I produced 38 research papers on fertilization, embryology and cellular physiology. I was elected vice president of the American Society of Zoologists in 1930. Who Am I?
   a. Lewis Howard Latimer
   b. Ernest E. Just
   c. Percy L. Julian

3. I graduate from Morehouse College in 1954. I earned my M.D. from Boston University in 1958. I was an instructor at Harvard Medical School and the New Jersey College of Medicine. In 1989, President George H. Bush named me head of the U.S. Department of Health and Human Services. Who Am I?

4. I received a medical degree from Boston University School of Medicine in 1897. In 1899, I joined the Boston University faculty and taught pathology, neurology and psychiatry for the next 40 years. I was one of the first Black American psychiatrists in the United States. Who Am I?
   a. Percy L. Julian
   b. Solomon C. Fuller
   c. Walter E. Massey

ANSWERS ON PAGE 116

5. I received a medical degree from McGil University in Montreal. I held a post at Columbia, Harvard, and Howard Universities. My pioneering work in the preservation of blood plasma saved the lives of countless soldiers and civilians during World War II. In 1949, I became head of the Department of Surgery at Howard University and chief of staff at Freedmen's Hospital. Who Am I?

6. In 1891, I founded the Provident Hospital and Medical Center in Chicago. My most notable contribution to medicine came in 1893, when I performed the first open-heart surgery. In 1913, the American College of Surgeons was formed, I was the only Black American among the 100 charter members. The U.S. Congress authorized a commemorative postage stamp in my honor in 1970. Who Am I?

7. This Black American physicist help develop the atomic bomb and the first nuclear reactor for atomic powered submarines in the 1930s. What is his name?

8. I did ground breaking work on syphilis, published the first medical textbook written by a Black American, "Syphilis and Its Treatment" published in 1936, remains a classic in the field. In 1949, I was awarded a clinical professorship at Harvard, becoming the first Black American professor in Harvard's history. Who Am I?

9. In 1968, this Black American acoustical engineer along with Gerhard Sessler invented the foil electrical microphone, that revolutionized the broadcast and telecommunications industries. What is his name?

10. This Black American, a kidney specialist with a medical degree from the University of Arkansas developed a technique for monitoring the blood supply to a transplanted kidney, making it possible for doctors to detect early signs of rejection. He was a professor of surgery at the Downstate Medical Center in Brooklyn, New York and surgeon-in-chief at Kings county Hospital. What is his name?
    a. Lloyd A. Hall
    b. James A. Harris
    c. Samuel Lee Kountz, Jr.

Answers on page 116

Answer Key

Black Inventors

1. a. Garrett A. Morgan
2. b. Frederick M. Jones
3. a. Richard B. Spikes
4. b. David N. Crosthwait, Jr.
5. a. Solomon Harper
6. b. Granville T. Woods
7. c. Lloyd A. Hall
8. a. Hubert Julian
9. Elijah McCoy
10. a. Lewis H. Latimer
11. c. J.M. Mitchell
12. a. G.B. Prather
13. a. George E. Carruthers
14. a. James A. Jones
15. c. Richard B. Spikes

Common Knowledge

1. 1920
2. 1919
3. 1934

Black Firsts

1. Edward Joseph Dwight, Jr.
2. Joycelyn Minnie Elders
3. Henry Aaron Hill
4. Shirley Ann Jackson
5. Phyllis Mae Daley
6. Dr. Levi Watkins, Jr.
7. Mae C. Jemison
8. Joseph H. Ward
9. St. Elmo Brady
10. Harvard Medical School
11. Samuel M. Nabrit
12. Colonel Guion S. Bluford, Jr.
13. Louis Tompkins Wright
14. Harvey Washington Banks
15. David Satcher
16. Helen Octavia Dickens
17. Justina Laurena Carter Ford
18. Jack E. White
19. David H. Blackwell
20. Roselyn Payne Epps

Who's Who

1. a. Meredith Gourdine
2. b. Ernest E. Just
3. Louis W. Sullivan
4. b. Solomon C. Fuller
5. Charles R. Drew
6. Daniel Hale Williams
7. Lloyd Quarterman
8. William Augustus Hinton
9. James West
10. c. Samuel Lee Kountz, Jr.

Music

Memorable Moments

1. In 1968, Jimi Hendrix had his first number one album. What was the title?

2. What was the first big song for the O'Jays in 1972?

3. The Commodores were formed in 1968 in Tuskegee, Alabama. True or False?

4. What was the first hit record for the Coasters in 1957?

5. In 1967, Bill Cosby had a hit record. What was the name of the record?

6. In 1963, Barbara Lewis had her first hit with what song?

7. Who sang, *I'm So Proud, It's All Right*, and *Amen*?

8. Maurice White is the lead singer for what group?

9. Cornelius Brothers & Sister Rose had their first hit in 1971 with what song?

10. Roberta Flack had her first big hit in 1972, with what song?

11. Who sang *Skinny Legs, Hold On To What You Got*, and *I Gotcha*?

12. Who sang, *Superstition* and *Living For The City*?

13. In 1971, Bill Withers had his first hit song, what was it?

14. Who sang, *Rock Steady, Spanish Harlem* and *Day Dreamin*?

15. What was Fats Domino's highest charted song?

16. What was the flip side of *Tears On My Pillow*, by Little Anthony and the Imperials?

Answers on page 135

17. This lead singer, on the Drifters smash hit *Save The Last Dance For Me*, went on to have solo hits of his own, including the smash hit *Stand By Me*. What is his name?

18. What was the first big song for the Marvelettes in 1961?

19. Booker T & The MG's had their first hit in 1962, what was the song?

20. Who was the one hit wonder with the big hit *Bare Footin*? .

21. In 1957, I sang this hit *Chances Are.* Who Am I?

22. The Vandellas sing backup on which early Marvin Gaye hit?

23. The B-side to Aretha's *Sweet Sweet Baby Since You're Been Gone* is considered by many to be her greatest performance. What is the name of that song?

24. I was Otis Redding co-writer on *I've Been Loving You Too Long, To Stop Now*, Who Am I?

25. On *A Fool In Love*, Ike Turner, known as a guitarist played what instrument?

26. Their hit single *End Of The Road*, stayed at number one on the pop chart for 12 weeks in a row. Name the group?

27. My classic hits include *You Send Me, Bring It On Home To Me* and *Only Sixteen*. Who Am I?
    a. Wilson Pickett
    b. Al Green
    c. Sam Cooke

28. I inherited the mantle of Sam Cooke and Otis Redding, sold more than 20 million records during the 1970s. Who Am I?

29. After what did the Isley Brothers name their record label T-Neck?

30. Ben E. King sang in what group prior to the Drifters?
    a. The Five Crowns
    b. The Platters
    c. The Moments

ANSWERS ON PAGE 135

Better Known As

Listed below are the names of some well known Black American singers on the left. Pick the name they are known by professionally on the right.

1.	Annie Mae Bullock	a. Tina Turner
2.	Ernest Evans	b. Harry Belafonte
3.	Otha Ellas McDaniels	c. Little Richard
4.	Ray Charles Robinson	d. Nat "King" Cole
5.	Steveland Morris	e. Muddy Waters
6.	Robert Calvin Bland	f. Jimi Hendrix
7.	Charles Edward Anderson	g. M.C. Hammer
8.	McKinley Morganfield	h. Blind Lemon
9.	Nathaniel Adams Coles	i. Bobby "Blue" Bland
10.	Stanley Kirk Burrell	j. Chubby Checker
11.	James Marshall	k. Billie Holiday
12.	Dana Owens	l. Leadbelly
13.	Hubbie Ledbetter	m. Diana Ross
14.	Lemon Jefferson	n. Queen Latifah
15.	Harold George	o. Chuck Berry
16.	Diane Ernestine	p. Stevie Wonder
17.	Ruth Jones	q. Ahmad Jamal
18.	Fritz Jones	r. Ray Charles
19.	Eleanora Fagan	s. Dinah Washington
20.	Richard Wayne Penniman	t. Bo Diddley
21.	Babe Kyro Lemon Turner	u. Blind Boy Fuller
22.	Edward Harrington	v. Guitar Slim
23.	Fulton Allen	w. Slim Harpo
24.	Eddie Jones	x. Black Ace
25.	James Moore	y. Eddy Clearwater

Answers on page 135

Dizzy Gillespie

Did You Know

That Dizzy Gillespie, born John Birks Gillespie, (October 21, 1917) Black American trumpet player, was the co-creator with alto saxophonist Charlie Parker, of Bebop or Modern Jazz. Gillespie started out on trombone at 14, but switched to trumpet. In 1932, he studied Theory at Laurinburg Institute in North Carolina. In 1956, Gillespie was invited to form a new big band by the U.S. State Department for a tour of Europe, as a musical good will ambassador. Gillespie is one of the most accomplished jazz musicians whose influence continues to this day. Dizzy died January 7, 1993.

MILESTONES

1. Ella Fitzgerald and Count Basie are the first Black Americans to win Grammy Awards in 1959.

2. Berry Gordy, Jr. establishes Motown Records in 1959, and Tamla Record labels in Detroit.

3. 1960, Chubby Checker launches a new dance craze with his number one hit record, *"The Twist."*

4. In 1971, Isaac Hayes's recording, *"Theme From Shaft",* is a number one pop hit. Hayes won an Oscar for his musical score of *Shaft.*

5. In 1971, Roberta Flack's *"The First Time Ever I Saw Your Face"* stays at the top of the pop carts for six weeks and wins a Grammy Award.

6. In 1984, Michael Jackson wins a record eight Grammy Awards for his 1983 album *"Thriller."*

7. In 1986, singers Ray Charles, Fats Domino and James Brown are among the first group of inductees into the new Rock n' Roll Hall of Fame.

8. In 1993, rhythm and blues singer Ruth Brown is inducted into the Rock n' Roll Hall of Fame. She popularized the 1950s with rhythm and blues tunes such as *"Mama, He Treats Your Daughter Mean", "Tear Drops From My Eyes"* and *"So Long."*

9. In 1946, jazz singer Sarah Vaughan wins *Downbeat* magazine's Female Vocalist of the Year Award. She continued to win this award every year through 1952.

10. Rev. James Cleveland, gospel singer and composer is know as the "Crown Prince of Gospel". During the 1950s and 60s, he composed over 500 songs. His most popular included *"Oh, Lord Stand By Me" "Walk On By Faith"* and *"He's Using Me"*

ANSWERS ON PAGE 135

THE GROUPS

1. This group was formed 1959, in Dayton, OH. The original members included: Billy Beck, Marvin Pierce, Jimmy "Diamond" Williams, Leroy "Sugar" Bonner, Marshall Jones, Clarence "Satch" Satchell, and Ralph "Pee Wee" Middlebrooks. The group enjoyed immense popularity during the mid 70s, they were the backing band for the Falcons, whose lead singer was Wilson Pickett. Two of the groups many hits are "*Skin Tight*" and "*Jive Turkey*." What is the name of the Group?

2. This group was formed 1957, in Chicago, IL. Their first hit was "*For Your Precious Love*" 1958, featuring Jerry Butler, follow by "*Gypsy Woman*" in 1961. What is the name of the group?
   a. The Impressions
   b. The Contours
   c. The Delfonics

3. Formed 1951, in Chicago, IL, original members of this group included: Paul Wilson, Jake Carey, Earl Lewis, Zeke Carey, Johnny Carter and Sollie McElroy. The group was consider to be one of the best during their era. They are remembered for their hit single "*I Only Have Eyes For You*." The group was inducted into the Rock n' Roll Hall of Fame in 2001. What is the name of the group.?

4. This group was formed 1957, in Detroit, MI, original members included: William "Smokey" Robinson, Bobby Rogers, Ronnie White, Pete Moore, and Claudette Rogers Robinson. Smokey Robinson is known as one of the premier songwriter in pop music. In 1961, he became vice president of Motown. In 1987, the group was inducted into the Rock and Roll Hall of Fame. What is the name of the group?

5. This group was founded by Maurice White, in Chicago, IL in 1969. "*That The Way of The World*" 1975, was the group's best album, as well as it's best selling. What is the name of the group?
   a. Earth, Wind & Fire
   b. The Temptations
   c. GAP Band

ANSWERS ON PAGE 135

6. This group was formed 1954, in Detroit, MI. The original members included: Renaldo "Obie" Benson, Levi Stubbs, Abdul "Duke" Fakir and Lawrence Payton. In 1994, the group celebrated four decades together, with the original members it started with. The group's 1965 hits included "*Ask The Lonely*", "*I Can't Help Myself –Sugar Pie Honey Bunch*" and "*Same Old Song"*. In 1990, the group was inducted into the Rock and Roll Hall of Fame. What is the name of the group?

7. Formed 1967, in New Orleans, LA, the original members of the group included: George Porter, Jr., Art Neville, Joseph Modeliste and Leo Nocentelli. Their hits included "*Sophisticated Cissy*", "*Look-Ka Py Py*", *Cissy Strut*" 1969, and "*Chicken Strut*" 1970. In November 2000, the group reunited for a one-night only concert, making it the first time in 20 years they all played together on the same stage. What is the name of the group?

8. This group was formed 1953, in Chicago, IL, the original members of the group included: Roebuck "Pop" Staples, Pervis Staples, Mavis Staples and Cleo Staples. Some of the group's hits were: "*Respect Yourself", "I'll Take You There*"-number 1 pop and R & B chart- "*If You're Ready-Come Go With Me*" and "*Let's Do It Again.* In 1999, the group was inducted into the Rock and Roll Hall of Fame. What is the name of the group?

9. This group was one of the most popular Black American groups of the '70s. Formed 1958, in Canton, OH, the original members included: Walter Williams, Eddie Levert, William Powell, Bobby Massey, and Bill Isles. All five members attended McKinley High School. The groups first name was the Triumphs, then the Mascots, in 1963, the group renamed themselves. They had eight number 1 Rhythm & Blues singles from 1972 to 1978, which included: "*Back Stabbers* 1972, "*Love Train*" 1973 and "*For The Love of Money*" 1974. What is the name of the group?

10. Formed in 1971, Oakland, CA this group original members included: Anita Pointer, Ruth Pointer, June Pointer and Bonnie Pointer. They became the first Black American women to play Nashville's Grand Ole Opry and the first pop group to perform at San Francisco's Opera House. Written by Anita and Bonnie Pointer "*Fairy Tale*" went to number 13 on the pop chart and won an Grammy as Best Country single of 1974. What is the name of the group?

 ANSWERS ON PAGE 135

11. Formed 1968, in Tuskegee, AL, the original members included: Lionel Richie, Jr., Milan Williams, Thomas McClary, Walter "Clyde" Orange, Ronald LaPread and William King, Jr. They met at a Tuskegee Institute talent show, when they were all freshmen. The group had several early hits, one of them being, "*Brick House*" in 1977. What is the name of the group?

12. Some of their hits included: "*Party Train*" 1983, "*Beep a Freak*" 1984, "*Going In Circles*" 1986, and "*I'm Gonna Git You Sucka*" 1988. Formed in 1970, in Los Angeles, CA, three brothers, Ronnie Wilson, Robert Wilson and Charles Wilson, natives of Tulsa, Oklahoma made up this group. What is the name of the group?
    a. The Isley Brothers
    b. O'Jays
    c. GAP Band

13. Formed in 1957, Detroit, MI, this group original members included: Pervis Jackson, George Dixon, Bobbie Smith, Henry Fambrough and Billy Henderson. The group started as the Domingoes, some of their hits include: "*I'll Be Around*" and "*Could It Be I'm Falling In Love*" 1972, "*The Rubberband Man*" 1976. What is the name of the group?

14. Kelly Rowland, Beyonce' Knowles, Letoya Luckett and Latavia Roberson, the four original members formed this group in 1989, in Houston, TX. What is the name of the group?
    a. The Pointer Sisters
    b. Destiny's Child
    c. Sweet Inspirations

15. This group was formed in 1959, in Detroit, MI, as The Primettes. Some of their biggest hits were: "*Stop In The Name of Love*", "*Back In My Arms Again*" 1965, "*You Can't Hurry Love*" and "*You Keep Me Hangin On*" 1966. In 1988, the group was inducted into the Rock and Roll Hall of Fame. What is the name of the group?
    a. Martha & The Vandellas
    b. The Supremes
    c. The Crystals

Answers on page 135

BLUES

After World War II, millions of Black Americans migrated from the rural South to large industrial cities in the North, such as Chicago and brought with them the traditional Blues of the Mississippi Delta, the music believed to be the true roots of all American music. It would be transformed into a new urban Blues by some of the greatest Blues artists.

1. This Blues musician helped import the rural music of the Mississippi Delta to Chicago in the 1950s, making possible the creation of the new Chicago Blues sound. Some of his hits include: "*Little Red Rooster*", "*Back Door Man*", *Killing Floor*" and "*Smokestack Lighting*". What is his name?

2. A Mississippi Delta legend, I was the most influential Blues man in the music's history. Who Am I?

3. I am known as the Queen of the Blues. Who Am I?

4. I am one of the most successful Blues man to emerge from the Memphis scene. Two of my biggest hits are "*Rock Me Baby*" and "*The Thrill Is Gone*". I became known as the "Beale Street Blues Boy", then "Blues Boy" and then simply who?

5. In 1948, this deep voiced Mississippi blues singer/guitarist enjoyed a hit with his first recording, "*Boogie Chillun*". He has been a major influence on Rock n' Roll. What is his name?

6. This Black American singer is known as the "Empress of The Blues". Her 1923 recording of "*Down Hearted Blues/Gulf Coast Blues*" sold 780,000 copies in six months and became the first million seller by a Black American singer. She recorded more than 160 songs, many of which she wrote. What is her name?

7. I was known as "The Godfather of Texas Blues." As a guitarist and lyricist, I had the uncanny ability to improvise words and music simultaneously. Born in Centerville, Texas, I spent my early years touring with rural blues legends, Texas Alexander and Blind Lemon Jefferson. "*Mojo Hand*" was one of my most commercially successful recordings. Who Am I?

ANSWERS ON PAGE 136

W. C. Handy House

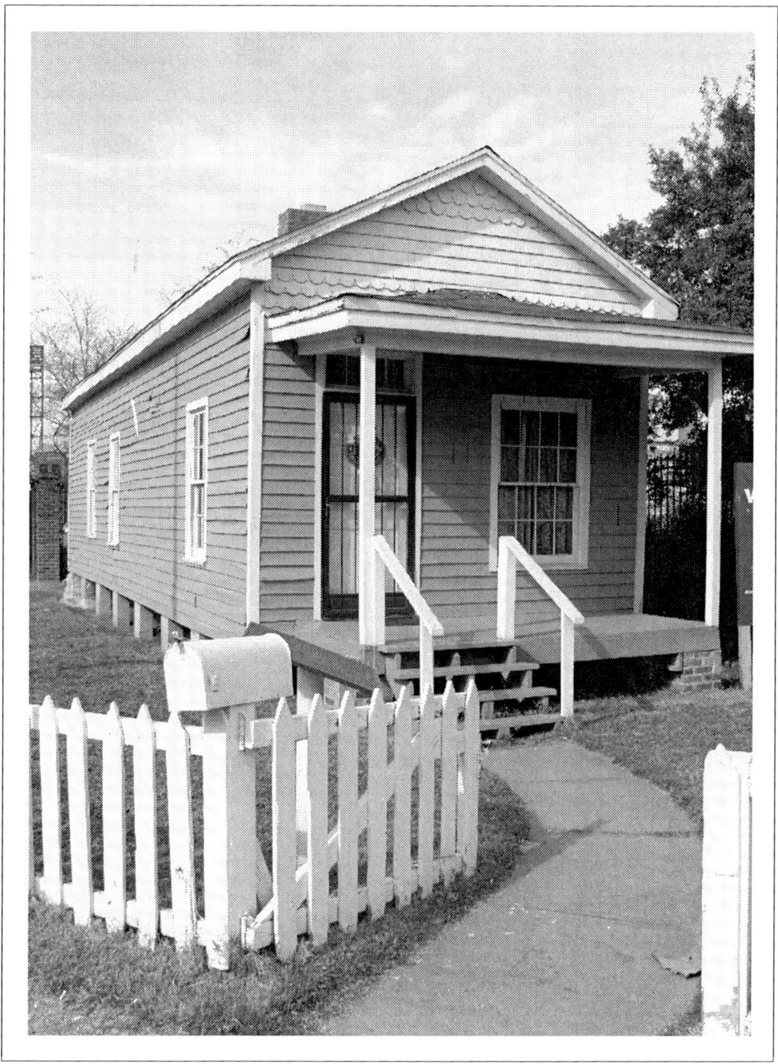

Did You Know

That W. C. Handy, known as "The Father of The Blues," in 1905, established his own band in Memphis, published such works as "*Memphis Blues*" "*Beale Street Blues*" and the world-famous "*St. Louis Blues*". He founded his own music publishing company in 1913, which he later moved to New York. Handy believed that true American music had sprung from music he heard from poor rural Black Americans of the Mississippi Delta country and made it his business to transcribe, perform and publish this music.

8. This Texas Blues guitarist and singer has been an inspiration to generations of blues musicians. Known as "The Master of The Telecaster," he relentlessly delivered the goods. Some of his recording are "*Frosty*," (his signature tune), "*Defrost*," and "*Ice Pickin*." Many consider "*Mastercharge*" to be his finest work. What is his name?

9. Born in Indianola, Mississippi, he is one of three guitar blues "Kings." He forged a style that is one of the most easily identified and widely copied in blues. In 1965, his signing with the Memphis based Stax Label, gave him hit after hit including "*Born Under A Bad Sign*," "*Crosscut Saw*." and "*Laundromat Blues*." What is his name?

10. Born 1918, in Richmond, Mississippi, he is one of the most powerful singers and guitarists in blues history, and certainly one of the most influential as well. Perhaps his greatest contribution to the music was the "Lick" he created for "*Dust My Blues*." Some of his others classics include "*Crossroads*," *Shake Your Moneymaker*," and "*Rollin' and Tumblin*." What is his name?

11. Born in Columbus, Georgia on April 26, 1886, she became recognized as one of the greatest female blues singers of the Classic Era. She sang blues as early as 1902, earning the title "Mother of The Blues" and leads a great tradition of women blues singers including, Bessie Smith, Big Mama Thornton, KoKo Taylor and many others. Some of the songs she put her name to are still in the blues repertoire, such as "*See See Rider*," "*Jelly Bean Blues*," and "*Stack O'Lee Blues*." What is her name?

12. Born in Vicksburg , Mississippi, it is impossible to imagine the post-war blues period without the presence and influence of this Chicago based blues songwriter, producer, bandleader and arranger. As a songwriter, he created countless hits for acts such as Muddy Waters, The Rolling Stones, Howlin' Wolf, KoKo Taylor and Cream just to mention a few. His credits include "*little Red Rooster*," "*Hoochie Coochie Man*,' "*Evil*," "*Mellow Down Easy*," "*Back Door Man*" "*Wang Dang Doodle,*" "*The Seventh Son*" and a host of other classics. What is his name?

ANSWERS ON PAGE 136

BILLIE HOLIDAY

DID YOU KNOW

That Billie Holiday was regarded by many as the greatest jazz singer ever recorded. Between 1935 to 1942, Holiday recorded her greatest work including, "*I Must Have That Man*", "*Am I Blue*", "*I Cried For You*" and "*I'll Get By*". Holiday also recorded her best known original, "*God Bless The Child*" which she help compose. Holiday died in New York City on July 17, 1959, she was only forty-four years old.

Ol' School
Classic Rhythm & Blues

1. This group was at their peak from 1955 to 1960, topping the charts with "*Twilight Time*", *My Prayer*" and "*Smoke Gets In Your Eyes*." What is the name of the group?

2. This singer/songwriter started out with Motown as the lead singer of the Miracles. He penned "*My Girl*" and "*The Way You Do The Things You Do*" for the Temptations. What is his name?

3. I got my first real break in 1969, with Harold Melvin and The Blue Notes, and went solo in 1976. On March 18, 1982, my Rolls Royce skidded across the road and crashed. The injuries I sustained left me paralyzed from the neck down. Who Am I?

4. Singer/actress, I started with the Supremes during the 1960s and went solo in 1970. My most popular albums include: "*Touch Me In The Morning*" and "*Silk Electric*." I was hailed for my role of Billie Holiday in the 1972 film *Lady Sings The Blues*. Who Am I?

5. One of the most important features of Rhythm and Blues was the development of the early groups, singing the close harmony that came to be known as what?

6. Vocalist and master of many instruments, I began recording with Motown at age 10. I had my first hit with "*Up-Tight Everything's Alright*" Who Am I?

7. This Black American Soul and Funk singer is known as *The Godfather of Soul, Soul Brother Number One, The Hardest Working Man in Show Business* and *Mr. Dynamite*. Who is he?

8. Alabama born singer and songwriter, I began my career with the Commodores and went solo in 1982. Who Am I?

9. Singer, Songwriter and producer, I am best known for the sound track of the 1972 film, *Superfly*. I was member of the Impressions before going solo. I combined music with political messages. Who Am I?

Answers on page 136

10. In 1958, "*Lonely Teardrops*". Written by my friend Berry Gordy, Jr. and Tyran Carlo became my first number one R & B hit. Who Am I?

11. "*There Goes My Baby*", written by the lead singer of this group, Ben E. King-under his real name Benjamin Nelson-went to number 2 on the chart in 1959. The group was inducted into the Rock n' Roll Hall of Fame in 1988. What is the name of the group?

12. The term Rhythm and Blues, also known as R & B came into vogue during the 1940s as an alternative to what term?

13. Some of my hits included: "*Can I Get A Witness*" 1963, "*I'll Be Doggone*" 1965, and "*Let's Get It On*" 1973. My album, Midnight Love which included "Sexual Healing" sold 2 million copies, which won a Grammy for Best Male R & B vocal performance. In 1987, I was inducted into the Rock and Roll Hall of Fame. Who Am I?

14. In addition to my numerous concert dates and TV appearances, I'm noted for my annual telethon benefiting the United Negro College Fund. Who Am I?

15. This group was formed in Detroit in 1961. They were the top male vocal group of the 1960s and early 70s, with hits such as "*Papa Was A Rollin Stone*", "*Get Ready*" and "*I Wish It Would Rain*". What is the name of the group?

16. This soul balladeer dies in a plane crash. He earned his place in music history with "*Sittin' On the Dock of The Bay*", "*I've Been Loving You Too Long*", and other hits. Who was he?

17. In 1966, "*What Becomes Of The Brokenhearted*" was a big hit for David Ruffin brother. What is his name?

18. On which early Marvin Gaye hit did The Vandellas sing backup?

19. "*If You Need Me*" song by Solomon Burke was this soul singer's first R & B hit. What is his name?

20. Remembering seeing "soul" written on the walls of burned out buildings in Detroit and elsewhere during the inner city riots of the 60s, Isaac Hayes decided to write "*Soul Man*". The song won a Grammy in 1968. Who did he write the song for?

Answers on page 136

21. In 1937, I recorded my first 78 LP for Decca Records, which included "*God Gonna Separate The Wheat From The Tares.*" I recorded over 30 albums in my career including 12, one million selling singles. I became known as the "Worlds Greatest Gospel Singer." Who Am I?

22. She was Motown's first big star, came to the attention of Berry Gordy as a 16 year old singer, pushing a song she'd written for Jackie Wilson. That song was "*Bye Bye Baby*," which became her first Motown hit in 1961. She teamed up with singer, writer, producer Smokey Robinson in 1962, scoring a string of hits including; "*The One Who Really Loves You*," "*You Beat Me To The Punch*," and "*Two Lovers.*" What is her name?
    a. Barbara Lewis
    b. Mary wells
    c. Irma Thomas

23. Born Eugene Dixon July 6, 1937, I am remembered by the Rock n' Roll audience almost solely for the classic doo wop soul ballad "*Duke Of Earl*," which went to number 1 on the pop and R&B charts in 1962. The record sold a million copies within a month of its November 1961, release. Who Am I?
    a. Curtis Mayfield
    b. Jerry Butler
    c. Gene Chandler

24. One of the sexiest singers on the Motown label, she is best known for her 1964, ballad hit "*Every Little Bit Hurts.*" she also recorded and co-wrote the original version of "*You've Made Me So Very Happy,*" which became a hit for Blood, Sweat & Tears. What is her name?

25. This singer will forever be associated with "*When A Man Loves A Woman*" 1966, a pleading soulful ballad he sang with convincing anguish and passion. Some of his other hits include; "*Warm and Tender Love*," and "*It Tears Me Up*" 1966, and "*Take Time To Know Her*" 1968. What is his name?
    a. Garnet Mimms
    b. Percy Sledge
    c. Solomon Burke

 ANSWERS ON PAGE 136

All That Jazz

1. I began playing alto sax at the age of 11, within two years I was playing baritone sax in the high school band. I am also known as "Yard bird," or "Bird." In November 1945, I recorded my first session as a leader, which included such classics as "*Billie's Bounce*," "*Ko-Ko*" and "*Now's The Time*." Who Am I?

2. He is the best known jazz musician in America. Trumpet player, educator, composer and artistic director of jazz at Lincoln Center, he was born October 18, 1961, in New Orleans. His father is a jazz pianist and teacher. What is his name?

3. Organist, I was born (1925) into a musical family in Norristown, Pennsylvania. I attended Hamilton School of Music in 1948, studying string bass and Ornstein School in 1949-1950, piano was my major. Some of my albums include "*Hobo Flats*," "*The Cat*," "*Peter and The Wolf*" and "*Walk On The Wild Side*." Who Am I?

4. I was the first guitarist to add to and modify the legacy lift to guitarists by Charlie Christian. In 1948, I was hired by Lionel Hampton as the band's guitarist. I am known as the top jazz guitarist of the 1960s, some of my classic jazz albums during the period of 1960-1963 include "*The Incredible Jazz Guitar*" 1960, and the live recording "*Full House*" 1962. Who Am I?

5. Composer and pianist in 1951, I made my concert debut with the Chicago Symphony Orchestra in a Mozart piano concerto at age 11. In 1973, I form a quartet, produced fusion's biggest selling record of all time, "*Headhunters*." Who Am I?

6. One of the most popular alto saxophonists of the early 1960s, I was born in Tampa, Florida, graduated from Florida A&M University. I taught and performed in Tampa and the Washington D.C. area. I played with Miles Davis (1958-1959), before launching my own successful quintet with my brother Nat. Some of the quintet's hits included "*This Here*" 1960, "*Mercy, Mercy, Mercy*" 1967 (penned by Joe Zawinul). Who Am I?

Answers on page 136

7. Guitarist and singer, I began playing guitar at the age of 11. I worked for a while in Jimmy Smith's Trio and recorded with many of music's best talent's, including Miles Davis. My 1975, album "*Breezin*" became a best seller. Who Am I?
   a. George Benson
   b. Quincy Jones
   c. Wes Montgomery

8. Born Ferdinand Joseph LaMenthe, composer and pianist. A seminal figure in early jazz, he introduced sophisticated harmonies and arrangements to what was considered Storyville Boredellos in 1902. He regarded himself as the inventor of Jazz, because he was among the first to write his jazz in musical notation, some jazz historians give his claim merit. He is known for tunes like "*Jelly Roll Blues*," "*New Orleans Blues*" and "*Black Bottom stomp*." Who was he?
   a. Jelly Roll Morton
   b. Cannonball Adderley
   c. Jimmy Smith

9. Jazz pianist, composer, I was one of the greatest of all jazz composers. My list of honors includes; 9 Grammy Awards for Achievement in the music industry; 16 honorary doctorates from such schools as Yale, Columbia and Brown; presidential medals from Johnson and Nixon and the NAACP's Spingarn Medal for achievement by Black Americans. Many of my songs are classics: "*It Don't Mean a Thing If It Ain't Got That Swing,*" "*Take The 'A' Train,*" "*Mood Indigo,*" and "*I got It Bad and That Ain't Good.*" My son, Mercer took over my band until his death in 1996. Who Am I?

10. Composer/arranger, I played trumpet with Lionel Hampton and Count Basie in the 1940s, I later turned to scoring films, such notable hits with soundtrack music to; "*In The Heat Of The Night,*" "*The Pawnbroker*" and many other films, writing themes for TV shows, and producing records for Michael Jackson, George Benson and others. As of 1997, I have been nominated for 97 Grammy Awards, winning 27. Who Am I?
   a. Wynton Marsalis
   b. Charlie Parker
   c. Quincy Jones

ANSWERS ON PAGE 136

Answer Key

Memorable Moments

1. *Ladyland*
2. *Back Stabbers*
3. True
4. *Searchin*
5. *Little Old Man*
6. *Hello Stranger*
7. The Impressions
8. Earth, Wind, & Fire
9. *Treat Her Like A Lady*
10. *The First Time Ever I Saw Your Face*
11. Joe Tex
12. Stevie Wonder
13. *Ain't No Sunshine*
14. Aretha Franklin
15. *Blueberry Hill*
16. *Two Kinds of People in the World*
17. Ben E. King
18. *Please Mr. Postman*
19. *Green Onions*
20. Robert Parker
21. Johnny Mathis
22. *Stubborn Kind of Fellow*
23. *Ain't No Way*
24. Jerry Butler
25. Piano
26. Boyz II Men
27. Sam Cooke
28. Al Green
29. Teaneck, New Jersey
30. The Five Crowns

Better Know As

1. a. Annie Mae Bullock
2. j. Ernest Evans
3. t. Otha Ellas McDaniels
4. r. Ray Charles Robinson
5. p. Steveland Morris
6. i. Robert Calvin Bland
7. o. Charles Edward Anderson
8. e. Mckinley Morganfield
9. d. Nathaniel Adams Coles
10. g. Stanley Kirk Burrell
11. f. James Marshall
12. n. Dana Owens
13. l. Hubbie Ledbetter
14. h. Lemon Jefferson
15. b. Harold George
16. m. Diane Ernestine
17. s. Ruth Jones
18. q. Fitz Jones
19. k. Eleanora Fagan
20. c. Richard Wayne Penniman
21. x. Babe Kyro Lemon Turner
22. y. Edward Harrington
23. u. Fulton Allen
24. v. Eddie Jones
25. w. James Moore

The Groups

1. The Ohio Players
2. The Impressions
3. The Flamingos
4. The Miracles
5. Earth, Wind & Fire
6. The Four Tops
7. Meters
8. The Staple Singers
9. The O'Jays
10. The Pointer Sisters
11. The Commodores
12. GAP Band
13. The Spinners
14. Destiny's Child
15. The Supremes

Blues

Blues

1. Howlin' Wolf
2. Robert Leroy Johnson
3. KoKo Taylor
4. B.B. King
5. John Lee Hooker
6. Bessie Smith
7. Sam "Lightnin" Hopkins
8. Albert Collins
9. Albert King
10. Elmore James
11. Ma Rainey
12. Willie Dixon

Ol' School

1. The Platters
2. Smokey Robinson
3. Teddy Pendergrass
4. Diana Ross
5. "Doo-Wop"
6. Stevie Wonder
7. James Brown
8. Lionel Richie
9. Curtis Mayfield
10. Jackie Wilson
11. The Drifters
12. Race Music
13. Marvin Gaye
14. Lou Rawls
15. The Temptations
16. Otis Redding
17. Jimmy Ruffin
18. *Stubborn Kind Of Follow*
19. Wilson Pickett
20. Sam and Dave
21. Mahalia Jackson
22. b. Mary Wells
23. c. Gene Chandler
24. Brenda Holloway
25. b. Percy Sledge

All That Jazz

1. Charlie Parker
2. Wynton Marsalis
3. Jimmy Smith
4. Wes Montgomery
5. Herbie Hancock
6. Julian "Cannonball" Adderley
7. a. George Benson
8. a. Jelly Roll Morton
9. Edward Kennedy "Duke" Ellington
10. c. Quincy Jones

Actors & Writers

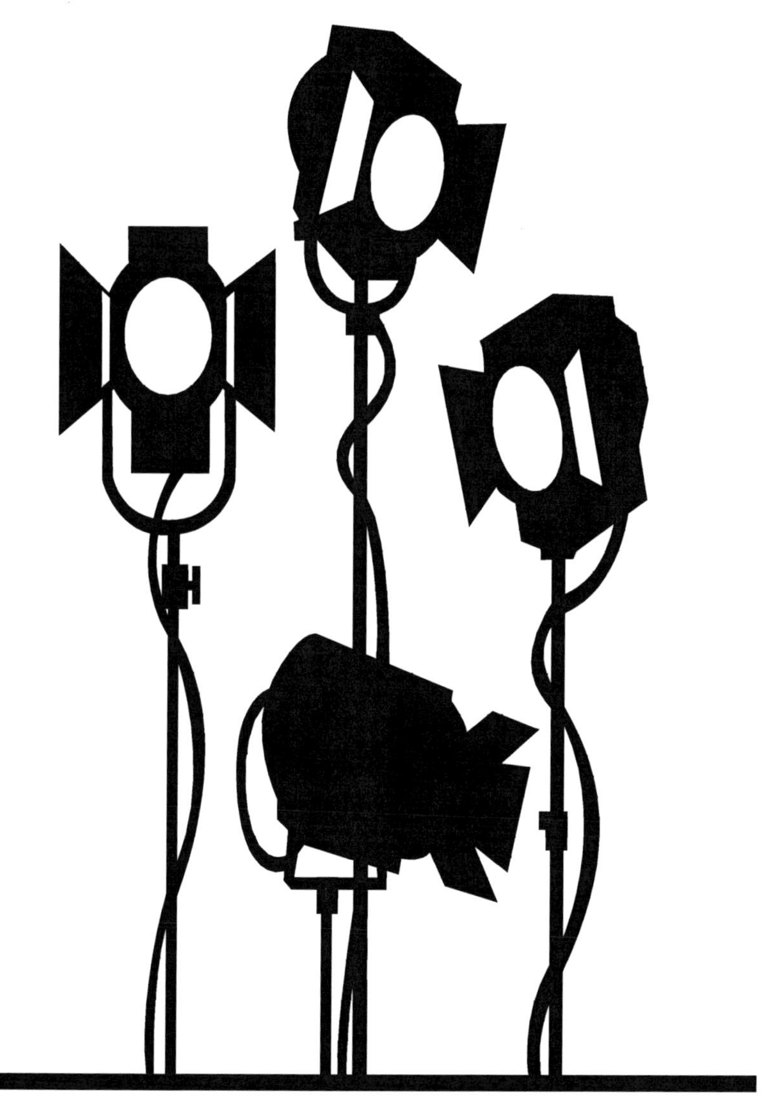

Black Movies

1. John Singleton directed this 1991, movie which starred Ice Cube, Cuba Gooding, Jr., Laurence Fishburne, and Angela Bassett. Name the movie
   a. Boyz N The Hood
   b. Rosewood
   c. Carmen Jones

2. Whoopi Goldberg, Danny Glover, Oprah Winfrey, and Margaret Avery starred in this 1985, movie directed by Steven Spielberg. What was the movie?
   a. Amistad
   b. The Color Purple
   c. Daughters Of The Dust

3. This 1971, movie directed by Gordon Parks, starred Richard Roundtree, and Moses Gunn. What was the movie?
   a. Shaft
   b. Buck and The Preacher
   c. Nothing But A Man

4. In 1989, I directed *Do The Right Thing*, which starred, Ossie Davis, Danny Aiello, Spike Lee, and Ruby Dee. Who Am I?
   a. John Singleton
   b. Spike Lee
   c. Ossie Davis

5. Samuel L. Jackson, Debbi Morgan, Diahann Carroll, Lynn Whitfield, Branford Marsalis, and Vondie Curtis-Hall starred in this 1997, movie directed by Kasi Lemmons. What is the name of the movie?
   a. Cabin In The Sky
   b. Eve's Bayou
   c. Claudine

6. Diahann Carroll and James Earl Jones starred in this 1974, movie directed by John Berry. Name the movie.

Answers on page 156

7. In 1970, I directed *Cotton Comes To Harlem*, which starred Ossie Davis, Godfrey Cambridge, and Calvin Lockhart. Who Am I?
   a. Spike Lee
   b. Sidney Poitier
   c. Ossie Davis

8. In 1972, I played Piano Man in *Lady Sings The Blues*, and earned an Academy Award nomination for my performance. I wrote and starred in *Bingo Long Traveling All Stars and Motor Kings* in 1976. Who Am I?

9. Morgan Freeman, Nigel Hawthorne, Djimon Hounsou and Anthony Hopkins starred in this 1997, movie directed by Steven Spielberg. Name the movie.
   a. Glory
   b. Amistad
   c. Carmen Jones

10. Esther Rolle, Elise Neal, Ving Rhames, and Don Cheadle starred in this 1997, movie directed by John Singleton. Name the movie.
    a. Rosewood
    b. A Raisin In The Sun
    c. Eve's Bayou

11. This 1993 movie, *What's Love Got To Do With It,* catapulted me into major stardom and won me rave reviews from critics. I won Golden Globe for my efforts as well as two NAACP Image Awards. In 1995, I starred in *Waiting To Exhale*, the box office hit based on a novel by Terry McMillan. Who Am I?

12. Denzel Washington, Angela Bassett, Delroy Lindo, Albert Hall, and Al Freeman, Jr. starred in this 1992, movie directed by Spike Lee. Name the movie.
    a. Lady sings The Blues
    b. The Color Purple
    c. Malcolm X

13. Danny Glover, Sheryl Lee Ralph, Vonetta McGee, Mary Alice, and Carl Lumbly starred in this movie, directed by Charles Burnett. Name the movie.
    a. Stormy Weather
    b. Daughters Of The Dust
    c. To Sleep With Anger

Answers on page 156

14. In 1972, Harry Belafonte, Sidney Poitier, Ossie Davis, and Ruby Dee starred in *Buck and The Preacher*. Who was the director?
    a. Spike Lee
    b. Sidney Poitier
    c. Gordon Parks

15. In 1971, Melvin Van Peebles directed and starred in this movie. Name the movie.
    a. Soul Food
    b. Up Town Saturday Night
    c. Sweet Sweetback

16. Diana Ross, Richard Pryor and Billy Dee Williams starred in this 1972 movie, directed by Sidney J. Furie. Name the movie.
    a. Lady Sings The Blues
    b. Nothing But A Man
    c. A Raisin In The Sun

17. Sidney Poitier and Ruby Dee starred in this 1961, movie directed by Daniel Petrie. Name the movie.
    a. A Raisin In The Sun
    b. Sounder
    c. The Learning Tree

18. This 1986, Spike Lee's film starred Spike Lee and Tracy Camilla Johns. Name the movie.
    a. Do The Right Thing
    b. She's Gotta Have I
    c. School Daze

19. This 1943, movie directed by Vincente Minnelli, starred Lena Horne, Eddie "Rochester" Anderson and Ethel Waters. Name the movie.

20. Dorothy Dandridge, Harry Belafonte, Brock Peters, Diahann Carroll and Pearl Bailey starred in this 1954, movie directed by Otto Preminger. Name the movie.
    a. Carmen Jones
    b. Sweet Sweetback
    c. The Color Purple

ANSWERS ON PAGES 156

Milestones

1. Despite initially poor reviews, *The Wiz*, (The Black American musical version of *The Wizard of Oz*), became a very successful show. It opened on Broadway on January 5, 1975, features an array of Black talented performers. *The Wiz* swept the Tony Award ceremonies in 1975 and became the longest-running Black musical in the history of Broadway with 1,672 performances.

2. In January 1972, Redd Foxx premiered on television as Fred Sanford in *Sanford and Son*, which remains one of the most popular syndicated shows.

3. Eddie Murphy made his first appearance on the television show *Saturday Night Live* on November 15, 1980.

4. On May 8, 1978, *Ain't Misbehavin'*, a popular Black American musical starring Nell Carter, Ken Page, Charlene Woodard, Andre DeShields and Armelia McQueen opened and played to Broadway audiences for 1,604 performances.

5. In 1964, Frederick O'Neal became the first Black American president of Actor's Equity. In 1970, he was elected international president of the Associated Actors and Artist of America.

6. In 1950, Sidney Poitier made his Hollywood screen debut in *No Way Out.*

7. In 1954, National Negro Network, the first Black American owned radio network in the United States, began broadcasting.

8. In 1959, Dorothy Dandridge win a Golden Globe Award for best actress in a musical for her role as Bess in *Porgy and Bess.*

9. In 1966, Bill Cosby star of *I Spy*, is the first Black American to win an Emmy for best actor in a dramatic series.

Answers on page 156

Sammy Davis, Jr.

Did You Know

That Sammy Davis, Jr. (December 8, 1925 - May 16, 1990), began performing with his father in Vaudeville acts by the age of four. Joined the Army in 1943, and served for two years directing shows and touring military installations. His 1966 autobiography "*Yes I Can*" was a bestseller. Davis starred in his own network television series, "The Sammy Davis Show" and Sammy & Company." His signature songs included "*Mr. Bojangles", "I've Gotta Be Me*" and "*What Kind of Fool Am I?"* In 1972 *"Candy Man*" went to the top of the charts.

Answers on page 156

BLACK ACTORS

1. I was nominated for an Academy Award as Best Actor for my inspired performance in *Driving Miss Daisy* 1989, and again in 1995, for my role in the *Shawshank Redemption.* Some of my film credits include: *Who Says I Can't Ride a Rainbow?* 1971; *Brubaker* 1980; *Eyewitness* 1981; *Harry and Son* 1984; *Clean and Sober* 1988; *Lean On Me, Phantom of The Mall, Driving Miss Daisy,* and *Glory* 1989; *The Shawshank Redemption* 1994; *Outbreak* and *Seven* 1995. Who Am I?

2. In 1995, I appeared in the films *Seven* and *When We Were Colored.* Some of my film credits include: *What Do You Say to a Nake Lady* 1970; *Shaft* 1971, *Shaft's Big Score!,* and *Embassy* 1972; *Shaft In Africa* 1973; *An Eye For An Eye* 1981; *City Heat* 1984; *Jocks* 1987; *Bad Jim* 1990; *A Time To Die* 1991; and *Lost Memories* 1992. Who Am I?

3. Some of my film credits include; *Boyz N The Hood* 1991, *Malcolm X* (I was cast as Betty Shabazz, wife of Malcolm X) 1992, *What's Love Got to Do With It* 1993, *Waiting To Exhale* 1995. Who Am I?

4. Singer, Actor, some of my film credits include: *Bright Road* 1953; *Carmen Jones* 1955; *Island In The Sun* 1957; *Odds Against Tomorrow* 1959; *Buck and The Preacher* 1972; *Uptown Saturday Night* 1974; and *White man's Burden* 1995. In 1992, I considered a bid for a Democratic seat in the New York Senate. Who Am I?

5. I played the lead role in the all Black cast of the film *Cabin In The Sky* 1943. Some of my film credit include: *What Price Hollywood?* 1932; *The Green Pastures, Show Boat* 1936; *Thanks For The Memory, Kentucky* 1938; *Gone With The Wind* 1939; *Love Thy Neighbor* 1940; *Cabin In The Sky* 1943; *It's A Mad Mad Mad Mad World* 1963. Who Am I?

6. Some of my film credits include: *A raisin In The Sun* 1961; *The Landlord* 1970; *The Skin Game* 1971; *The Laughing Policeman* 1973; *The White Dawn* 1974; *An Officer and A Gentleman* 1982; *Jaws* 1983; *Enemy Mine* 1985; *Iron Eagle* 1986; *The Principal*

ANSWERS ON PAGE 156

1987; *Iron Eagle II* 1988, and *Iron Eagle III* 1992. I won a Best Supporting Actor Academy Award, for my role as the tough drill sergeant in the 1982, film *Officer And A Gentleman.* Who Am I?

7. I received an Oscar award for Best Supporting Actress in *Gone With The Wind* in 1940. Some of my film credits include: *Judge Priest* 1934; *The Little Colonel* 1935; *Showboat* 1936; *Saratoga* 1937; *Gone With The Wind* 1940; *The Great Lie* 1941; *In This Our Life* 1942; *Johnny Come Lately* 1943; *Since You Went Away* 1944; *Margie* 1946; *Never Say Goodbye* 1946; *Family Honeymoon* 1948; and *The Big Wheel* 1949. Who Am I?

8. I won an Oscar for Best Supporting Actress for *Ghost* in 1990. Some of my film credits include: *The Color Purple* 1985; *Jumpin' Jack flash* 1986; *Fatal Beauty* 1987; *The Telephone, Clara's Heart* 1988; *The Long Walk Home, Kiss Shot, Ghost* 1990; *Sister Act* 1992; *Made In America,* and *Sister Act II* 1993. Who Am I?

9. Singer, actress, some of my film credits include: *Variety Girl* 1947; *Isn't It Romantic?* 1948; *Carmen Jones* 1955; *St. Louis Blues* 1958; *Porgy and Bess* 1959; *The Landlord* 1970; and *Norman...Is That You?* In 1971, I hosted my own TV variety show. Who Am I?

10. I Hold a Ph.D. in education and I'm very active in the affairs of the Black American community. Actor and comedian, some of my film credits include: *Man and Boy* 1972; *Uptown Saturday Night* 1974; *Let's Do It Again* 1975; *Mother Juggs and Speed* 1976, *California Suite* 1978; and *Ghost Dad* 1990. Who Am I?

11. A actor and comedian, some of my film credits include: *The Last Angry Man* 1959; *The Trouble Maker* 1964; *The President's Analyst* 1967; *Bye Bye Braverman* 1968; *Watermelon Man, Cotton Comes To Harlem* 1970; *The Biscuit Eater* 1972; *Whiffs* 1975; and *Scott Joplin* 1977. I was stricken with a fatal heart attack on the set of the TV movie *Victory At Entebbe*, in which I played the role of Uganda President Idi Amin. Who Am I?

12. Some of my film credits include: *Nothing But A Man* 1964; *The Great White Hope* 1970; *Shaft* 1971; *Shaft's Big Score* 1972; *Amazing Grace* 1974; *Cornbread Earl and Me* 1975; *Ragtime* 1981; *Firestarter* 1984; *Heartbreak Ridge* 1986; and *Dixie Lanes* 1988. I died of asthma complications at the age of 64. Who Am I?

Answers on page 156

13. In 1976, I was elected to the Board of Governors of the Academy of Motion Picture Arts and Sciences. Some of my film credits include: *Dr. Strangelove* 1964; *The Comedians* 1967; *The Great White Hope* 1970; *The Man* 1972; *Claudine* 1974; *The Bingo Long Traveling All Stars and Motor Kings* 1976; *Star Wars* (voice of Darth Vader only) 1977; *Conan The Barbarian* 1982; *Return of The Jedi* (voice only) 1983; *Coming To America* 1988; *The Hunt For Red October* 1990; and *Jefferson In Paris* 1995. Who Am I?

14. In 1989, I co-starred with Eddie Murphy in Harlem Nights. A comedian, actor and director, I'm the recipient of five Grammys, for my millions selling comedy albums. Some of my film credits include: *The Busy Body* 1968; *Wild In The Streets* 1969; *Lady Sings The Blues* 1972; *Uptown Saturday Night* 1974; *Silver Streak* 1976; *Greased Lighting* 1977; *Stir Crazy* 1980; *Some Kind Of Hero, The Toy* 1982; and *Brewster's Millions* 1985. Who Am I?

15. Actor and director, I made history when my portrayal of an obliging handyman in *Lilies Of The Field* 1963, won me an Academy Award for Best Actor. Some of my film credits include: *No Way Out* 1950; *The Blackboard Jungle* 1955; *Edge Of The City* 1957; *Porgy and Bess* (as Porgy) 1959; *A Raisin In The Sun, Paris Blues* 1961; *Lilies Of The Field* 1963; *In The Heat Of The Night, To Sir With Love, Guess Who's Coming To Dinner* 1967; *Buck and The Preacher* (also directed) 1972; *Uptown Saturday Night* (also directed) 1974; *Let's Do It Again* (also directed) 1975; and *A Piece Of The Action* (also directed) 1977. Who Am I?

16. Actress and singer, some of my film credits include: *Carmen Jones* 1954; *Porgy and Bess* 1959; *Paris Blues* 1961; *Hurry Sundown* 1967; *Claudine* 1974; and *The Five Heartbeats* 1991. In 1984, I joined the cast of the TV series "*Dynasty*". Who Am I?

17. In 1970, I turned out my first film as director with, *Cotton Come To Harlem*. My wife, Ruby Dee and I are active in Civil Rights and humanitarian causes. Actor, director, producer, playwright and screenwriter, some of my film credits include: *No Way Out* 1950; *Fourteen Hours* 1951; *The Joe Louis Story* 1953; *The Cardinal* 1963; *Shock Treatment* 1964; *The Hill* 1965; *A Man Called Adam* 1966; *Sam Whiskey, Slaves* 1969; *Let's Do It Again* 1975; *School Daze, Do The Right Thing* 1988; *Jungle Fever* 1991; and *Grumpy Old Men* 1993. Who Am I?

Answers on page 156

18. Tap dancer, musician, actor and songwriter, I made several films during the 1980s': including *Cotton Club* 1984 and *Tap* 1989. My performance as Jelly Roll Morton in *Jelly's Last Jam* earned me a Tony Award in 1992. Who Am I?
    a. Gregory Hines
    b. Danny Glover
    c. Ossie Davis

19. Actor and singer, I won a scholarship to Rutgers and graduated as a four letter man, holder of a Phi Beta Kappa key and fluent in more than 20 languages. I was considered one of the best offensive tackles ever to play college football. Some of my film credits include: *Body and Soul* 1925; *The Emperor Jones* 1933; *Song of Freedom* (UK); *Show Boat* 1936; *King Solomon's Mines* (UK) 1937 and *Tales of Manhattan* 1942. Who Am I?
    a. Bill Cosby
    b. Paul Robeson
    c. Morgan Freeman

20. I received much praise for my portrayal of a brutal pivotal character in *The Color Purple* 1985. Some of my film credits include: *Out* 1982; *Witness, Silverado* 1985; *Lethal Weapon* 1987; *Lethal Weapon 2, Dead Man Out* 1989; *Grand Canyon* 1991; *Lethal Weapon 3* 1992 and *Bopha!* 1993. Who Am I?
    a. James Earl Jones
    b. Danny Glover
    c. Richard Pryor

Answers on page 156

Josephine Baker

Did You Know

That Josephine Baker, international celebrity, outspoken opposition to discrimination was the first and greatest Black American dancer to emerge in the genre now called performance art. In 1927, Baker was earning more than any other entertainer in Europe. She also starred in two movies in the early thirties; "*Zou - Zou*" and "*Princess Tam - Tam*." In 1953, while on a Far Eastern tour she adopted the first two of 12 orphans of various nationalities, her "Rainbow Tribe." On April 8, 1975, Baker opened at the Bobino Theater in Paris to an enthusiastic audiences and great reviews. Josephine Baker died on April 12, 1975, in Paris.

Answers on page 156

BLACK MUSICALS

From 1961, to the mid 1980s were one of the most active periods for Black American performers in musical theater. Many of the Black musicals produced during these years, have enjoyed significant runs both on Broadway and off Broadway stages, as well as extended road tours.

1. This Langston Hughes' musical opened on Broadway December 11, 1961. It was directed by Vinette Carrol. Although the musical ran for only 57 performances on Broadway, it went on to tour extensively throughout the United States and abroad. What is the name of the musical?
   a. Black Nativity
   b. The Wiz
   c. Dreamgirls

2. Despite initially poor reviews, this Black American musical became a highly successful show. It opened on Broadway January 5, 1975. The musical swept the Tony Award Ceremonies in 1975, and became the longest running Black musical in the history of Broadway with 1672 performances. What is the name of the musical?
   a. Shuffle Along
   b. The Wiz
   c. Ain't Misbehavin'

3. Leslie Uggams and Robert Hooks appeared in this Black American musical, which opened in New York on April 26, 1967. The musical looked at five decades of Black history, received a Tony Award and ran for 293 performances. What is the name of the musical?
   a. Hallelujah Baby
   b. Bubbling Brown Sugar
   c. Raisin

4. On May 23, 1921 this musical opened on Broadway, signaling the return of Black American musicals and the arrival of the Harlem Renaissance on the American stage. The musical featured the talented singer-dancer Florence Mills. What is the name of the musical?
   a. Carmen Jones
   b. Green Pastures
   c. Shuffle Along

 ANSWERS ON PAGE 156

5. This musical, based on Ossie Davis' 1961 play *Purlie Victorious*, opened May 9, 1979 with Meba Moore and Robert Guillaume in lead roles. What is the name of the musical?
   a. *Purlie*
   b. *The Wiz*
   c. *Jelly's Last Jam*

6. In 1964, I dazzled Broadway in this Clifford Odets' musical, *Golden Boy*. I was supported by a cast which included Louis Gossett, Jr., Billy Daniels, Robert Guillaume, and Lola Falana. The musical ran for 586 performances. Who Am I?

7. Virginia Capers, Helen Martin and Joe Morton opened this musical, based on Lorraine Hansberry's play *Raisin In The Sun*. The play opened on October 13, 1973. It received the Tony Award for the best musical in 1974, and had a run of 847 performances. What is the name of the musical?

8. This popular Black American musical of the 1970s, opened on May 8, 1978. Based on a cavalcade of songs composed by Thomas "Fats" Waller, this musical starred: Nell Carter, Ken Page, Armelia McQueen, Andre DeShields and Charlene Woodlard. It Played on Broadway for 1,604 performances. What is the name of the musical?

9. This Black American musical opened at the Imperial theater on December 20, 1981, captivated Broadway audiences with a cast that included Loretta Devine, Cleavant Derricks, Jennifer Holiday, and Cheryl Alexander. It ran for 1,522 performances on Broadway and had an extensive road tour. Jennifer Holiday won a Tony Award for her role as Effie Melody White. What is the name of the musical?
   a. *One Mo' Time*
   b. *Dream Girls*
   c. *Bring In 'da Noise, Bring In 'da Funk*

10. On April 27, 1986 Debbie Allen opened in the lead role of this musical. Reviews were favorable and the musical enjoyed a run of 386 performances. What is the name of the musical?
   a. *Sweet Charity*
   b. *Bubbling Brown Sugar*
   c. *Eubie!*

ANSWERS ON PAGE 156

Black Firsts

1. I became one of the first Black American women to direct a production on Broadway in 1972. I directed the Broadway hits: *Don't Bother Me, I Can't Cope* 1972; *Your Arms Too Short To Box With God* 1976; and *When Hell Freezes Over I'll Skate* 1979. Some of my many honors are an Emmy Award, an Obie Award, three Tony Award nominations, the New York Outer Critics Circle Award, and induction into the Black Filmmakers Hall of Fame. Who Am I?

2. During the 1960s, I became the first Black American to choreograph dances at the Metropolitan Opera. Some of my major works include: *Haitian Suite II, Bal Negre, Spirituals* and *Anabacoa*. Who Am I?
   a. Katherine Dunham
   b. Vinnette Carroll
   c. Alice Childree

3. Actress, singer and choral director, in 1949 I became the first Black American to win a Tony Award for my performance as Bloody Mary in the Broadway production of *South Pacific*. Who Am I?

4. Playwright, actress and director, I became the first Black American woman to receive an Obie Award in 1955, for my off Broadway production of *Trouble In Mind.* I have written several novels including: *Like One Of The Family, Conversations From a Domestic's Life* 1937; *A hero Ain't Nothin' But a Sandwich* 1973. Who Am I?
   a. Alice Childress
   b. Juanita Hall
   c. Lorraine Hansberry

5. Bill Picket, Lawrence Chenault, Anita Bush, Steve Reynolds and thirty Black American cowboys starred in the first all Black Western movie, *The Crimson Skull*, also known as *The Scarlet Claw*. This silent black and white movie was filmed on location in what all Black American town in Oklahoma?
   a. Rentiesville
   b. Boley
   c. Redbird

Answers on page 156

6. What was the name of the first full length Broadway musical written and performed in 1903, by Black Americans? The show played to packed houses at the New York Theatre on Broadway, until it left for London, where it played at the Shaftesbury Theatre.
   a. In Dahomey
   b. The Wiz
   c. Purlie

7. The first successful TV variety show hosted by an Black American was aired on NBC television from 1970 to 1974. The show won a Emmy in 1970, for outstanding writing of a variety show. The host of the show performed in the sketches, his roles include Reverend Leroy, the pastor of the church of "What's Happening Now" and Geraldine. What was the name of the show?
   a. "The Cosby Show"
   b. "The Flip Wilson Show"
   c. "Sanford and Son"

8. In 1975, this Black American hosted this CBS nationally televised game show, "Musical Chairs." Unfortunately the show was cancelled after one season. Who was the host?

9. Known as the first Black American prima ballerina in America to perform at the Metropolitan Opera Company, I attended Los Angeles City College and the Los Angeles Art Center School. I am also an accomplished painter. From 1950 to 1951, I was lead dancer in Cole Porter's musical *Out Of This World* which won me the Donaldson Award. Who Am I?
   a. Pearl Primus
   b. Janet Collins
   c. Katherine Dunham

10. In 1970, Charles Gordone became the first Black American playwright to win the Pulitzer Prize for drama. The play was a story about a Black petty hustler and saloon owner who tried to elude the local Mafia. What was the name of the play?
   a. "No Place To Be Somebody"
   b. "A Raisin In The Sun"
   c. "Fences"

ANSWERS ON PAGE 156

COMMON KNOWLEDGE

The following achievements and/or events all occurred in the same year. Can you identify the year?

1.

- Alice Childress's play "*Moms*" based on the life of Jackie "Mom" Mabley is staged off Broadway.
- The action film "*Lethal Weapon*" is released, starring the popular cop buddy team of Danny Glover and Mel Gibson
- "*Hollywood Shuffle*," was written, produced and directed by Robert Townsend, starring Keenen Ivory Wayans, Anne-Marie Johnson, Helen Martin, Craigus R. Johnson and Paul Mooney.

The year was: 1987 1989 1992

2.

- Whoopi Goldberg wins an Academy Award as best supporting actress for her role in "*Ghost*"
- Charles R. Johnson wins the National Book Award for his novel "*Middle Passage*."
- Selby Steele publishes his "The Content of Our Character," which wins the National Book Critics Circle Award.

The year was: 1986 1990 1994

3.

- Angela Bassett and Laurence Fishburne starred in the film "*What's Love Got To Do With It*," a film about the life of Tina Turner.
- President Clinton presents theatrical director Lloyd Richards, entertainer Cab Calloway and singer Ray Charles with the National Medal of The Arts Awards.
- Actor Sidney Poitier wins the National Black Theatre Festival's Living Legends Award.

The year was: 1989 1990 1993

 ANSWERS ON PAGE 156

Black Writers

1. I am best known for my autobiography, "*Coming of Age In Mississippi*" 1968, which received the Best Book of The Year Award from the National Library Association in 1969. Who Am I?

2. In 1976, I became the first Black American to be appointed a consultant in poetry at the Library of Congress. Who Am I?

3. In 1944, I was a reporter for the *Daily World* in Atlanta, GA. I became the first Black American correspondent to be admitted to a White House press conference, which I attended on February 8, 1944. Who Am I?

4. Novelist and short story writer, I was born in Chicago on April 13, 1891. In 1930, I became the first Black American women to win a creative writing award from the prestigious Guggenheim Foundation. Who Am I?

5. Journalist, Novelist and editor, in 1931, George Schuyler's published his first novel. What is the title of the novel?

6. This 1977, book sold more than 8.5 million copies, was translated into 26 languages, and won 271 different awards. The Pulitzer Prize and National Book Award committees honored its contribution to American history. ABC turned it into an eight part television series. Name the author and the title of the book.

7. In 1970, the first book in the autobiographical series on the life of Maya Angelou was published. What is the title of the book?

8. In 1990, this writer wins the National Book Award for his third novel, "*Middle Passage*". He is the first Black American since Ralph Ellison to win the award. Who is the author?
   a. Alex Haley
   b. Charles Johnson
   c. Richard Wright

Answers on page 156/157

9. I am best known for my award winning story of Black American life, "*A Raisin In The Sun*" 1959, the first play written by a Black American woman to be produced on Broadway. Who Am I?

10. "*Native Son*" was the first work by a Black American to be offered by the Book-Of-The-Month Club. What is the author's name?

11. In 1900, Charles Chesnutt's first novel was also the first Black American novel to be offered by a major publishing house. What is the title of the book?

12. Gwendolyn Brook's second book of poetry published in 1950, won the first Pulizer Prize ever awarded to a Black American, man or woman author, in any category. What is the title of the book?

13. This author's first novel, "*Home To Harlem*" (1928), describes the urban adventures of a railroad cook named Jake Brown. It was the first novel by an Black American to make the best seller list in New York City. What is the author's name?

14. I was the first Black American playwright to have a nonmusical production on Broadway, "*The Chip Woman's Fortune*" (1923). Who Am I?

15. Fiction writer, journalist and editor, I published my first novel, "*The Living Is Easy*" in 1948. Who Am I?

16. Name the Black American playwright and novelist who portrayed the court case that ended school segregation in his play "*A Land Beyond The River*"

17. I am the first Black American woman to win the Nobel Prize in Literature. My major novels include "*Sula*" 1973, "*Tar Baby*" 1981, "*Beloved*" 1987, and "*Paradise*" 1998. Who Am I?

18. I have written novels, poetry, essays, autobiography and children's books. I am best known for my 1982, Pulitzer Prize winning novel, "*The Color Purple*," which was made into a successful film. Who Am I?

19. "*Before the Mayflower*," was published in 1962. What is the author's name?

ANSWERS ON PAGE 157

20. I am widely acclaimed for both my poetry and essay collections. I was selected to compose and read the poem "*On The Pulse of Morning,*" for the 1993, Inauguration of President Bill Clinton. Who Am I?

21. This Mississippi born novelist is known for her wide range of subject matter and narrative technique. Some of her major works include *"The Women of Brewster Place,*" "*Bailey's Cafe,*" "*Mama Day,*" and *"Linden Hills,*" What is her name?

22. This Los Angeles based Black American writer of selective fiction is best known for his Easy Rawlins series. His major works include "*Devil In A Blue Dress,*" "*A Red Death,*" "*Black Betty,*" and "*White Butterfly.*" What is the author's name?
    a. Walter Mosley
    b. Langston Hughes
    c. Harry S. Hayden

23. This Black American author is one of the giants of American literature and a master of many genres. His poetry collections include "*The Weary Blues*" (1926), *"Fine Clothes To The Jew*" (1927), "*Montage of A Dream Deferred*" (1951), and "*The Panther and The Lash*" (1967). What is his name?
    a. Charles Johnson
    b. Langston Hughes
    c. Richard Wright

24. Some of this playwright's major works include "*The Brownsville Raid*" (1976), "*Zooman and The Sign*" (1979), and "*A Soldier's Play,*" winner of a 1982 Pulitzer Prize. What is the author's name?
    a. Charles H. Fuller, Jr.
    b. George Herriman
    c. Ralph Waldo Ellison

25. I am best known for "*Invisible Man,*" a 1952, novel that won me a National Book Award. Who Am I?
    a. Ralph Waldo Ellison
    b. Toni Morrison
    c. Maya Angelou

ANSWERS ON PAGE 157

ANSWER KEY

BLACK MOVIES

1. a. *Boyz N The Hood*
2. b. *The Color Purple*
3. a. *Shaft*
4. b. Spike Lee
5. b. *Eve's Bayou*
6. Claudine
7. c. Ossie Davis
8. Richard Pryor
9. b. *Amistad*
10. a. *Rosewood*
11. Angela Bassett
12. c. *Malcolm X*
13. c. *To Sleep With Anger*
14. b. Sidney Poitier
15. c. *Sweet Sweetback*
16. a. *Lady Sings The Blues*
17. a. *Raisin In The Sun*
18. b. *She's Gotta Have It*
19. *Cabin In The Sky*
20. a. *Carmen Jones*

BLACK ACTORS

1. Morgan Freeman
2. Richard Roundtree
3. Angela Bassett
4. Harry Belafonte
5. Eddie "Rochester" Anderson
6. Louis Gossett, Jr.
7. Hattie McDaniel
8. Whoopi Goldberg
9. Pearl Bailey
10. Bill Cosby
11. Godfrey Cambridge
12. Moses Gunn
13. James Earl Jones
14. Richard Pryor
15. Sidney Poitier
16. Diahann Carroll
17. Ossie Davis
18. a. Gregory Hines
19. b. Paul Robeson
20. b. Danny Glover

BLACK MUSICALS

1. a. *Black Nativity*
2. b. *The Wiz*
3. a. *Hallelujah Baby*
4. c. *Shuffle Along*
5. a. *Purlie*
6. Sammy Davis, Jr.
7. *Raisin*
8. *Ain't Misbehavin'*
9. b. *Dream Girls*
10. a. *Sweet Charity*

BLACK FIRSTS

1. Vinnette Carroll
2. a. Katherine Dunham
3. Juanita Hall
4. a. Alice Childress
5. b. Boley
6. a. *In Dahomey*
7. b. "The Flip Wilson Show"
8. Adam Wade
9. b. Janet Collins
10. a. "No Place To Be Somebody"

COMMON KNOWLEDGE

1. 1987
2. 1990
3. 1993

BLACK WRITERS

1. Anne Moody

Black Writers

2. Robert Earl Hayden
3. Harry S. McAlpin
4. Nella Larsen
5. *Black No More*
6. Alex Haley - *Roots*
7. *Why The Caged Bird Sings*
8. b. Charles Johnson
9. Lorraine Vivian Hansberry
10. Richard Wright
11. *The House Behind The Cedars*
12. Annie Allen
13. Claude McKay
14. Willis Richardson
15. Dorothy West
16. Loften Mitchell
17. Toni Morrison
18. Alice Walker
19. Lerone Bennett, Jr.
20. Maya Angelou
21. Gloria Naylor
22. a. Walter Mosley
23. b. Langston Hughes
24. a. Charles H. Fuller, Jr.
25. a. Ralph Waldo Ellison

Index

E

F

G

H

I

J

K

L

M

M

N

O

T

U

Order Form

Send me _____ copy/copies of "The Black History Quiz Book; A look Back At The 20th Century" at $12.95 ea.

....$ ________
Plus shipping..$3.00 ea $________
Please send check or money order..Total $ ________
Make payable to Melvett Chambers

Please Print or Type

Name: ____

Address: ____

City: ____________________ State __________ Zip ____________________

Please send order to: Melvett Chambers
P.O. Box 165
Hennepin, OK 73444

Book will be shipped within 24 hours of receipt of payment.

Contact us at: 580-868-2357, email: melvettc@tds.net, fax: 580-868-2358
or visit our website at: www.melvettblackhistory.com

Order Form

Send me _____ copy/copies of "The Black History Quiz Book; A look Back At The 20th Century" at $12.95 ea.

....$ ________

Plus shipping...$3.00 ea $________

Please send check or money order...Total $ ________

Make payable to Melvett Chambers

Please Print or Type

Name: ____

Address: ____

City: ________________________ State __________ Zip ____________________

Please send order to: Melvett Chambers
P.O. Box 165
Hennepin, OK 73444

Book will be shipped within 24 hours of receipt of payment.

Contact us at: 580-868-2357, email: melvettc@tds.net, fax: 580-868-2358
or visit our website at: www.melvettblackhistory.com